For my

parents

# ESSAYS

For

# CIVIL SERVICES

and

Other Competitive Examinations

How to approach and write on any new topic in the examination hall

20 Demonstrative Essays & 20 Suggested Topics of high relevance

PULKIT KHARE

arihant

Arihant Publications (India) Limited

ARIHANT PUBLICATIONS (INDIA) LIMITED



**卐 Administrative & Production Offices**

**Corporate Office:** 4577/15, Agarwal Road, Darya Ganj, New Delhi -110002
Tele: 011- 47630600, 23280316; Fax: 011- 23280316

**Head Office:** Kalindi, TP Nagar, Meerut (UP) - 250002
Tele: 0121-2401479, 2512970, 4004199; Fax: 0121-2401648

**All disputes subject to Meerut (UP) jurisdiction only.**

**卐 Sales & Support Offices**

Agra, Ahmedabad, Bengaluru, Bhubaneswar, Chennai, Delhi (I&II), Guwahati, Haldwani, Hyderabad, Jaipur, Kolkata, Kota, Lucknow, Nagpur, Meerut, Patna & Pune

**卐 ISBN**

978-93-51410-22-5

**卐 Price : ₹ 125**

**PO No. :** TXT-59-T057791-3-24

Typeset by Arihant DTP Unit at Meerut

Printed & Bound in India
by Arihant Publications (India) Limited

For further information about the products from Arihant,
log on to www.arihantbooks.com or email to info@arihantbooks.com

# PREFACE

The idea to present a book on **Essay** writing stuck me while I was arranging my notes after the success in Civil Services Examination 2010. During my previous successful attempts, I had composed several write ups as part of mock practice sessions before the mains examination. I had also been approached by several friends and aspirants asking for my notes and compositions after the results. It is then that I decided to compile my hand written compositions for the benefit of the aspirants. The consistent decent scores in the Essay paper of this examination give me confidence to advice and guide the aspirants about the requirements of this paper.

The idea behind presenting an un-edited version of essays is to show the true level of output in simulated examination conditions. They showcase the methodologies of approaching an essay paper, which includes framework preparation and presentation skills, to create a logical, coherent and effective composition.

I believe that essay writing is all about expression of ideas and have cherished the experience of composing right from my school days. As an examination paper, a little planning, practice and smart presentation can yield additional valuable marks which ultimately have a bearing on the rank of candidate. The target has been to develop this book as a one-stop-solution for all needs of the essay paper.

The blessings of Almighty, support of my family and their faith in my abilities and perseverance to keep chasing my dream have been the driving forces behind my successful endeavors. I consider this compilation as my little contribution to the student community.

I would also like to this opportunity to express my gratitude to **Arihant Publications (India) Limited,** Meerut. Their cooperation in bringing out this book has been immense.

I hope the book manages to simplify the approach to Essay paper, clear the myths surrounding the art/science of Essay writing, helps in fetching better scores for candidates and brings them the desired success. Awaken the passion to excel.

*BEST WISHES*

***Pulkit Khare***

# CONTENTS

## Part C Develop Better Writing Skills

### List of Topics for Practice

1. Outsourcing : *Trends and Impacts*
2. The Dignity of Labour
3. Third World Industrialization
4. Millennium Development Goals : *The Road Ahead*
5. Life of an Illegal Immigrant
6. Corporate Social Responsibility in India : *Evolution and Performance*
7. Streets of My City
8. Habit is Second Nature
9. Reuse Reduce Recycle
10. A Woman in an Indian Metropolitan
11. Growing Intolerance in the Society
12. Wikileaks and the Age of Transparency
13. An Eye for an Eye
14. Tax Avoidance and Tax Havens : *Undermining Democracy*
15. Life of an Anti Corruption Protest
16. The Difficult Indian Neighbourhood
17. The Right to Dissent
18. Unlocking the Potential of Microfinance
19. We Live in Deeds, not in Years
20. Naxal Menace : *The War Within*

# ABOUT *the* BOOK

It is easy to say that this book is different from the conventional essay writing books. Every author could brag about being unique in his content and presentation. However, the real judge of the utility and uniqueness of the book can only be the reader. The author hopes that the approach to essay writing in a competitive examination scenario illustrated in this book evicts positive response from the readers.

Unlike other essay books, this is not a mere collection of "edited" essays. The essays here serve a demonstrative purpose to the approach illustrated in the first segment of the book. The author aims to guide the students through the mental process of composing an essay in the examination conditions.

## PART A

The book sets forth the guidelines about approaching any new topic for composing an essay in the examination hall. Through elementary mental steps and of neglected aspects of presentation, the author wishes to simplify the approach to this paper. It is the approach to which the experience and success of author stands testimony.

The author believes that the core of essay writing is all about expressing oneself on given topic. Any reasonably informed person would be able to carry out that act perfectly. However, beyond that core ability of putting words to paper lays the refinement of art of expression. There is also need to present this coherent logical write up under the constraints of the time limit. It is here that the book attempts to guide the readers from experiences of the author.

One need not run after individual topics during essay preparation as the topics one encounters in the examination hall will be entirely new. Thus, effort and time should not be wasted in attending coaching classes or purchasing numerous books on essay. This book aims to teach fishing, rather than serve a prepared fish. The essays in the book are only for demonstrative purpose, which exemplify the approach described in Part A of the book.

# PART B

The book presents a compilation of 20 un-edited essays written by the author. The purpose is to highlight the methodology of part A along with presenting a level of writing sufficient to fetch decent marks in this examination.

The essays manage to touch varied domain and points can be picked up from these by the candidates. These essays were written in strict examination condition by the author during the time of preparation. The write ups presented in the book are un-edited products of authors approach to a novel topic. The purpose behind this format is to demonstrate the level of writing which manages to fetch decent marks from the point of view of examination. The edited products in other books fail to give idea to the readers about the actual level of essays written by the successful candidates in this examination.

Often, the student remains under impression that successful candidates write something unique and that their own expression is subpar. The anxiety related to this exam often creates self doubts in the mind of the student regarding the level of his writing and presentation. There is desire to gauge their writings against the one composed by the successful ones. It is here that this book might help the aspirants by scrutinizing these un-edited products. It also manages to quench the curiosity about what successful candidates produce to fetch better marks in the paper.

The mind space of students is also clouded by several self doubts about the level of their grammar, method of their presentation, dearth of ideas at disposal for the topic, standards of their handwriting, etc. This negative mindset inhibits their free flowing expression of thoughts and reflection of their potential onto paper, failing to fetch the deserving marks. It also takes them from one book to another and from one coaching to other, leading to wastage of time and effort. I believe that essay paper need not be the cause such headaches. I hope this book serves as a one stop solution for all the queries and worries related to the Essay paper.

# PART C

Part C of the book gives a list of suggested topics which can be used to practice the approach described in Part A and demonstrated in Part B. Mock essay writing sessions on these topics under simulated examination conditions will generate self confidence in the student on ability to compose on a novel topic.

The author wishes to simplify the process of approaching and attempting the Essay paper in the examination. This paper can be easily utilized to earn a solid score which can have a marked influence in determining the rank, career and eventually life of the student. It is just a matter of few marks in such competitive examinations which count for a lot. And if these few notches could be scaled in the essay paper with a little planning, calibrated approach and practice, it is definitely worth the effort.

The author believes that competencies and skills lie hidden in each one of us. It is only the matter of polishing those skills as per the requirements of the Civil Services Examination. This book is an attempt in that pursuit.

Unleash your potential.

*Best Wishes*

# Part A

# Approach to Essay Writing

# Decoding the **Art/Science *of* Essay Writing**

*The first man who used the term **essai** (a French word meaning **attempt**) was a Frenchman, **Michel de Montaigne**, who wrote about his feelings on certain ideas like idleness, agony, etc in the late 1500s. A few years later, and in the early 1600s, **Sir Francis Bacon**, the first English essayist, wrote on subjects like death, ear, friendship, studies. As a composition, the essay presents the opinion or analysis of writer on a particular subject. Literally, the word means **an attempt** or **an experiment** and the information supplied by the Concise Oxford Dictionary is that in essay is a literary composition on any subject, usually in prose, and short.*

However, all this information is of little use when one is tasked with composition of an essay. The matters become grave when the writing is judged on several criterions in a competitive examination. It requires a dedicated and systematized planned approach. The write up must reflect a logical flow of ideas, touching all domains of the topic with an appropriate beginning and conclusion. Though a lot can be said about the requirements from an essay in this examination, the basic premise can be grasped from the **Gazette** and the **Question Paper**.

The Essay question paper of the Civil Services Examination itself states *Examiners will pay special attention to the candidate's grasp of his material, its relevance to the subject chosen and to his ability to think constructively and to present his ideas concisely, logically and effectively.*

The Gazette states *Candidates will be required to write an essay on a specific topic. The choice of subjects will be given. They will be expected to keep closely to the subject of the essay to arrange their ideas in orderly fashion and to write concisely. Credit will be given for effective and exact expression.*

These sources serve as the most authentic authority regarding the requirements from the content and presentation in an Essay paper. There is no need to look beyond these for any guidance or help. The practice process for the essay paper should be modeled accordingly by the candidate to imbibe these requirements in his writings. The candidate must grasp the need of being methodical rather than abrupt and wayward in his expression of ideas. It may be tough initially, but a little practice in a set format illustrated later, will drive in the requisite discipline to fetch better scores. The approach illustrated later can be easily inculcated into habit through practice. Through suitable examples from the essays illustrated in Part B of the book, the author highlights every step of composing a scoring write up. Along with content, some effort on the presentation front may also reap rich dividends.

*The entire process in the examination hall can be practically categorized into three phases :*

1. **Preparation**
   - Weeding
   - Dissection
   - Regulated Brainstorming
   - Plotting
2. **Presentation**
3. **Revision**

# 1 PREPARATION

*One must utilize the minutes before distribution of question paper in preparing neat margins on the answer sheet. Also, the last 2 pages of the sheet can be titled as "rough work" and should be cancelled out after finishing the essay. These are used in the preparation of the mental maps (explained later).*

## Weeding

Just like in gardening, so in essay writing, weeding forms a critical groundwork to prepare for a beautiful product. It involves scanning of topics in the question paper and making the selection of the topic. However, most often, it is the process of "rejection" of those topics which are not falling in one's zone of comfort.

It is essential to boil down to 2 probable topics at the end of this step (Step 1). At times, after few minutes of **Dissection** (Step 2), one may realize that the choice of topic needs to be reconsidered. It is then that one can revert to the topic considered as second best in this step.

Go sequentially from one topic to another. There will be a topic or two which may immediately spark an ignition in your mind and seem temptingly **do-able**. There will be others which will be instantaneous put off, sparking an immediate repulsion. One can and should trust their instinct in this preliminary scanning of topics.

The "do-able" need further respect and due consideration. I believe one needs to be patient at this step and devote some seconds to each topic sorted out. There must be several factors which must be considered at this stage. It is always better to opt for a topic about which one has either read sufficiently either in graduation, post-graduation or as optional for this examination. It subconsciously adds to the confidence, which finds a positive reflection in the writing. Also, the session of **Regulated Brainstorming** (explained later), helps in digging out the details from the bank of sub conscious memory in such topics. However, there may be instances where none of the topics served by the examiner satisfies the above requirement. In such scenario, maintaining calm is absolutely essential to judge the **select ability** of the topic.

*Analyze a topic in backdrop of following mental queries :*

**1.** *Do I understand each word of the topic individually and the topic holistically?*

**Example** Preparing Indian society for global leadership (Essay No. 1) talks about social preparedness more than any other aspect. Hence the focus must be on social indicators, their evaluation and progress. It can touch economic, cultural, political aspects but only to the extent that they influence the social indicators and society preparation. In the bigger picture, these have to be viewed in context of global leadership- the need, the demands and the progress.

**2.** *Do I understand the sub parts into which a topic can be broken?*

**Example** Role of media in maintaining communal harmony (Essay No. 20) does not demand a general view on media and its growing role. It can be broken into major sub-parts as: *Role of media* and *Maintenance of communal harmony*. Each sub-part need to be understood in totality and then the various angles of the relation between subparts should be explored. Firstly, the roles of different types of media in society must be analyzed, followed by the need and relevance of communal harmony in society. Then, a linkage must be established highlighting media's role in reporting instances of communal clashes, preventive role that media can play and the sensitivity that media must display in such precarious situations.

**3.** *Am I comfortable with the broad category to which this topic belongs?*

**Example** *Role of Education in Development* (Essay No. 15) or *Women's Reservation as a Means of Women Empowerment* (Essay No. 5) fall primarily in ambit of social sector themes. However, the topic like *e-Governance* (Essay No. 3) or *Building India into Knowledge Society* (Essay No. 4) demands a level of comfort with scientific developments. The use of terminology and choice of words suitable for a particular broad theme help in enhancing the effect of any write up. A person comfortable with science or humanities would be able to conjure up more ideas for a topic in that field and would be able to explain them more effectively. Similarly, attempting an essay belonging to the domain of one's optional subject also helps in better and effective expression.

**4.** *Do I have sufficient quantity of content from which I can sustain about 1200-1800 word write up, without being repetitive?*

Firstly, one will have to do a quick memory refresh about having encountered this topic earlier at some stage of preparation. Secondly, one will need to mentally visit the **7 domains of brainstorming** (discussed later) and check if each can deliver sufficient content for the given topic.

The topic zeroed in after these considerations must be the one which generates confidence and falls in the comfort zone of the individual. Never try to go for a **different topic** in attempt to fetch marks. The topic may appear to be **very common** and one "which in likelihood is selected by the majority of candidates". These thoughts should not cross the mind of the student even once. One should focus on one's strength and not think about the world in this examination. Often, the strategy to **be different** and choosing a **unique** topic backfires badly. Marks will follow your answer sheet even on a **common topic** if your content is strong and striking.

## Dissection

Break the chosen topic of the essay into segments wherever possible and spread it on paper (as illustrated). Take up each segment of the broken topic and focus on it separately.

**Example** Consider the topic, *Globalisation and WTO : An Era of Neo-imperialism*, which can be dissected into Globalisation, WTO and neo-imperialism. Now each of these sub parts can be subjected individually to the next step (*7 Domains of Brainstorming*) to collect sufficient thoughts for writing. After jotting these, the relations of the dissected sub parts can be analyzed in detail.

## Regulated Brainstorming

An exercise which is easier said than done. All management compendiums swear by its importance but how to apply it in those critical minutes of the examination hall is **a different ball game** altogether. There are discourses on its utility but no one ever tells the procedure to do it. We are told to explore the various facets of the topic under scanner and to broaden the dimensions of our thinking. Teachers ask us to jot down **anything that comes to the mind** related to the topic in the process.

In the examination condition, the student is operating under limitation of time. One needs to **regulate** the process to deliver fruitful results rather than embarking on a hunting expedition in wilderness. Often, one tends to jot down much which has to be cancelled later as being unfit to be put in the final draft. This result in wastage of crucial minutes spent in putting those unwanted thoughts on the rough sheet initially and considering them for inclusion in final draft later on. There is need to drive in precision and efficiency in the process of brainstorming by smartly regulating the process. Hence there is a need of a **regulated brainstorming**. The regulations are essential as we are focused on a purpose of writing a concise, logical and effective draft within the limitations of the examination time.

### 7 Domains of Brainstorming

1. Who, What, When, Where and How
2. Evolution of the topic
3. The contemporary reasons of being discussed
4. Cause and Effect
5. Social, Cultural, Political, Economical, Religious angles (if any)
6. Local, National and International domains
7. Scrutiny of subject in backdrop of constitutional values : Democracy, Socialism, Sovereignty

*These domains will help in regulating the process of brainstorming in the wilderness.*

## Plotting

This activity is a sub part carried out concurrently or just after the exercise of "regulated brainstorming". It involves preparation of a rough mental sketch of the sequence in which the sub parts of the topic have to be presented in the logical lay out.

After the session on 7 domains of brainstorming culminates, immediately come out of the mental involvement in sub parts. Have a re-look at the topic in totality. On the mind map sheet produced after "regulated brainstorming", start putting numbers deciding the order in which the essay will "flow" on the answer sheet. Be logical in deciding the order. Put numbers like 1,2,3,4,... on the prepared mind map to broadly decide the sequence of picking and explaining the sub part. The sub parts must follow in a connected manner; else they will give a fragmented look to the essay. This highlights the importance of this step.

Remember, plotting is a **rough** exercise and must be regularly revisited while finishing writing on a particular segment. In the first plotting (*after "regulated brainstorming" and prior to commencing writing*) broadly set the flow of essay. However, be mentally flexible in deviating from this initial plotting. After writing a first few paragraphs, one will normally have a mental intuition about the logically ensuing segment. One should then have a re-look at the initially plotted order and bring adjustment accordingly. (*Say, a sub part marked 4 can be skipped and taken after writing 5 and 6, if the student feels that logical flow of essay demands such adjustments.*)

# 2 PRESENTATION

*All the preparation comes to a naught, if the execution fails to deliver the desirable. After the groundwork has been successfully done, it is time to develop the blueprint into an effective document. Remember, it is the final presentation on the paper which the examiner judges and basis his marks upon. Hence, in spite of a calibrated planning, a neat execution is critical to the vaunted success.*

*Apart from the content, which is the soul of the essay, several other elements add up to a perfect write up. These include*

## Vocabulary

It does help to have familiarity with a better range of words to pick and choose from while framing one's expressions. A better vocabulary coupled with a right sense of usage helps in neater articulation of thoughts on paper. However, one must stay guard that the essay answer sheet is not a place to display the wizardry of words. The focus is on apt articulation.

A **Decent Level of Vocabulary**, which can be enriched over the time of preparation even without much extra effort, is sufficient to tide over the essay paper smoothly. The depth and flow of ideas expressed must immediately attract and grasp the attention of the examiner. Often, if the focus is on displaying the mastery of words, the content takes a backseat, which is **detrimental to the marks** expected from the paper. One can easily put oneself in the shoes of the examiner and imagine the scenario. No one would appreciate a write up which is decorative with heavy words but fail to register any impression with the content.

There is little need to run after building vocabulary as it will only distract one from the core preparation for the exam. The habit of extensive reading, which is a positive bye product of the preparation for this examination, takes care of the automatic strengthening of vocabulary. This happens when the extensive reading is done in an **active** mode by being aware of the words being encountered in the process. "Active" reading involves smart use of dictionary to register words rather than skipping over them. This would automatically contribute to a sub conscious strengthening of the wide range of words at one's command. One must be appreciatively aware of the usage of words and phrases done in editorials and articles and keep a mental note of it.

## Paragraphing

*A paragraph is a series of sentences, arranged in a logical order, dealing with one idea or topic. The sentences in a paragraph support and develop a central idea. Thereby, each sentence should have an unmistakable bearing on the one before it. The sentences must cohere to give an impression of an integrated mass free from any discordant note. One sentence must melt or flow into another with the force of a persuasive logic. Each paragraph should similarly flow into next to create the composition. Do not frame long endless paragraphs. Try and maintain a sense of uniformity in the length of paragraphs. The paragraphs may vary from "x" to "y" lines depending on the content taken up in the paragraph. Try to restrict the expansion of any particular point to a single paragraph. However, in case the point needs more explanation, be at liberty to explain it in 2 similar sized paragraphs.*

*This norm about length of paragraphs should be relaxed for the first and the last paragraphs of your essay, which are generally lengthier than the others. The introductory paragraph can be broken into few smaller paragraphs to make it more effective and impactful.*

## To Quote or Not to Quote

It is a commonly asked query whether one should start an essay with a quote or not. No rule book orders an essay to mandatorily begin with a quotation. However, if one happens to remember an apt quotation, one should not hesitate to begin with that. Do not put quotation just for the sake of having one.

The knowledge of quotations which fit in the context displays an aptitude for richness and perfection of content in an individual. It definitely showcases a better read individual who has put in effort to link his wide reading to the presentation of the matter. However, for those with not a wide taste of reading, a little smart work can still reap dividends.

This smart work needs to be done in advance during the period of your preparation for examination. While doing your one's readings of newspaper /magazine/optional, whenever one comes across a good quotation, one should make an effort to note it down in a separate note book. One can supplement this collection with any standard book of quotations. However, one must avoid falling in the **trap of plenty**. I believe that one should have a command over few than an idea about plenty when it comes to quotations for the purpose of essay writing in this examination. It is the selection of these few which makes all the difference.

Get a grasp of a few *all weather quotations* and their *smart use* will definitely reap good dividends. Such quotations have wider range in terms of their subjective interpretations and thus, can be used in multiple contexts. Make these quotations part of your note book and revise them frequently to master them. The next step is their smart use in the context of the given essay topic. A careful study of the essays in this book will further impress this point on the students.

**Example** *Arise, awake and stop not till the goal is reached* is a classical exhortation by Swami Vivekananda which stands for action, inspiration, positivity, development and determination. Smart contextual use of this equation can be done in several varied topics dealing with these basic themes.

**Illustration 1**

***I have begun two of the essays demonstrated in the book with the same quotation. It happens to be one of my favourites.***

*Where the mind is without fear and the head held high,*
*into such heaven, my father, let my nation awake.*

Essay No. 12 on **Indian Democracy** and Essay No. 5 on **Women's Reservation as a Means of Women Empowerment** open with this **all-weather** quotation. However, the ensuing paragraph manages to garb the same quotation with the requisite contextual relevance and thereby leads into different topics all together.

Centre align any quotation on the answer sheet. Leave a two line margin on top and bottom of quotation to make your quotation stand out from the rest of the text of the essay. It is not essential to know the speaker of the quotation being used. One must only mention it in case of 200% surity, else it can be safely avoided.

Illustration 2 ***I have begun the Essay No. 17 on "Social Networking" with this quotation.***

*"What is this life, so full of care?*
*We have no time, to stand and stare."*

*However, since I was not sure about the poet in this case, I have safely omitted any mentioning of names.*

## Facts and Figures

Do not make your essay answer sheet appear as a ledger book by an **unflinching devotion** to facts and figures. Often, due to intensity of preparation for this exam, one tends to remember several statistics and develops a habit of quoting them at the drop of hat. This display of mastery over figures needs to be curtailed in the essay examination.

The presentation of essay demands a logical and structured flow of ideas. The logic may be qualitatively advanced through arguments than by **quantitative reliance on statistics.** I believe that figures may be quoted to strengthen one's arguments but not in every instance. Their use should be balanced and spread evenly across the write up. Say, the use of numbers and percentages in a few paragraphs continuously to highlight few facets of topic and their complete neglect later on will make their use lop sided. In such cases, if possible, during plotting the 7 domains of brainstorming, do create sufficient gap in the order of taking up these domains. This will prevent crowding of factual information and lend a balance to the essay in terms of facts and figures usage.

The write up will touch several facets of the topic and each would demand a convincing flow of ideas. After going through the 7 domains of brainstorming, one will realize that not every domain be necessarily be justified by use of numbers. In fact, the presence of too much numerals and percentages may hinder the flow of ideas and display a weak expressive ability of the student. It may present a fragmented look to the write up.

In a series of thoughts and explanations, figures can be used to highlight certain stark realities but they remain weak without an ensuing binding analysis. The focus should be on the inferences one draws from these statistics. Using them sparingly, at places where they accentuate the argument, is justified. It is their balanced use, as per the topic of essay, which will earn some credit.

For those who have trouble remembering facts and figures, life is much simpler. One should not worry about their inclusion in the essay write up. It is the content, with or without the **crutches of numerals**, that constitutes a good essay.

One word of caution is must before winding up this segment: It is better not to quote a statistic than quoting a drastically wrong one. Similarly, quoting data from a reputable survey by a national or international body is acceptable, but one must be 200% sure about the quoted source and the values.

Often, the query regarding use of sketches, flowcharts and diagrams also baffles the students. I believe that these tools of presentations should be avoided as far as possible. These tools portray a weakness in the expressive ability of the student with the usage of words. They may appear visually attractive, but their potency in fetching marks remains questionable.

### Handwriting

*I will not be diplomatic in saying that good hand writing is not necessarily a mark fetcher. It does help in bettering the first impression. However, to sustain the favourable effect of good hand writing in the mind of the examiner, it must be backed by an equally impressive content. Since, major changes in handwriting cannot be achieved overnight, one must ensure a bare minimum of legible handwriting. Also, be slow and try to deliver your best writing efforts in your first 1-2 pages by controlled writing. By that time, the strength of your content would have aroused interest in the examiner and he will not mind the deterioration in handwriting.*

*Try to avoid cuttings and corrections. It does not leave a good impression on the examiner. Be extra cautious about this in the first 2-3 pages where you create an impression about yourself through your words. In the latter pages, if unavoidable, make a neat cutting using a single line running across the mid height of the text.*

## Punctuations

The art of correct usage of punctuations imparts a **definite** and **clear meaning** to the write up. The correct usage of *comma, full stops, semi colon, colon, dash, inverted comma, exclamation sign, interrogation sign, apostrophe and hyphen* gives a good impression about the candidate to the examiner. It tells about the grasp of candidate on the basics of English grammar. It is always better to be correct in the usage of punctuations. A grammatically and structurally correct sentence adds clarity to the meaning of a sentence.

## Subtitling & Underlining

I think this breaks the flow of essay and would not prescribe the use of subtitling. The breaking of title done in mental maps need not be reflected on final draft in form of subtitling. This, I believe, would give a fractured look to the write up. Instead, sparing use of underlining can be effective means of drawing attention of the examiner to the basic theme of the paragraph. Do not over underline, in which case, the process would lose its' relevance. Selective underlining of the key words in a paragraph is a critical oft-neglected exercise. One must exercise judiciousness, discretion and sensibility in this process as the underlined portion draws the attention of the examiner and becomes a window for him to explore and judge your essay. This step can also be taken up during the phase of revising the essay with the help of a pencil.

**Illustration**

*Essay 1 has been presented with selective use of underlining as done in the exam paper.*

## Parenthesis

At times, when one wishes to elaborate or give some additional information about something in a sentence, the use of parenthesis can be done. They can be either in form of comma, dashes or brackets.

**Illustration**

1. *The responsibilities, both of an individual and a nation, have grown in face of diminishing isolated and growing terror.*
2. *Indian society has traditionally been a patriarchal society -- a society where men turned the financial wheels and women were confined to drive the household wheels.*

## Abbreviations

We are accustomed to the use some abbreviations as a matter of routine. Note making in the classrooms is different from presentation of essay. We need to **unlearn** the use of routine abbreviations. Learn to separate standard abbreviations from non standard ones. Avoid using non-standard abbreviations like **bk** (*for book*), **bldg** (*for building*), **b/w** (*for between*), **mkt** (*for market*), **hr** (*for hour*), **prg** (*for programme*), **trg** (*for training*), **dev**. (*for development*), **eco**. (*for economy*) etc. Their use would indicate a casual approach of the candidate towards the essay paper. However, standard abbreviations like UNICEF, WHO, UN, SAARC, RBI when used repeatedly need not be expanded each time. One may expand them in brackets, when used for the first time, if one is confident about being correct.

## 3 REVISION

*Try and finish writing your essay 15 minutes prior to the allotted time limit. The final 15 minutes can be used to quickly skim through the essay. Utilize this revision time to underline the prominent segments of the essay. This step of revision also allows for correction of spelling mistakes, which may have inadvertently crept in during the flow of writing. It is also the time to have one final look to correct any grammatical or punctuation errors in the write up.*

*The importance of this step lies in the satisfactory feeling of* **holistic completion** *one experiences, after having gone through the entire write up and putting in a few alterations.*

## Time Division

It is essential to keep track of time in the examination hall. Timing different segments of your essay gives a mental discipline and ensures justice to each element. The timings suggested are approximate and can have minor adjustments as per individuals. Through some mock practice tests one can develop the knack of sticking to these time limitations.

| Step | | Time |
|---|---|---|
| **Preparation** | | |
| | Weeding | 10 min |
| | Dissection | 2 min |
| | Regulated Brainstorming | 20 min |
| | Plotting | 5 min |
| **Presentation** | (Introduction + Body + Conclusion) | 128 min |
| **Revision** | | 15 min |

After stepwise going through the entire process of creating a logical, precise and effective composition in the examination hall, it is essential to have a broader look at the major segments of the write up. For the gallery of critiques, no essay writing session can be imagined without a discourse on the **conventional** parts of an essay. It is essential to be aware of the requirements from these segments to enable one to perform a wholesome evaluation of the essay.

# Introduction

*Well begun is half done* rightly said and this applies to our essay also. The trickiest aspect of essay writing is about striking the right chord with an apt beginning. Struggling to find the best beginnings is very natural.

At times, I have ended up spending about 20 minutes to come up with a suitable first line. It is a teasing experience, where one will be toying with a number of ideas and their apt framing to form that **perfect** first sentence.

However, one must be patient at this step and devote sufficient time to satisfy oneself. Remember, this first paragraph is introducing you to the examiner and first impressions do carry significant weightage. This first paragraph should gradually lead one into the topic.

I would advise not to hit the topic straightaway in the first 1-2 sentences. Rather one should have a small build up in these introductory sentences. However, by the time of winding up this slightly lengthy (*or split*) first paragraph, one should have set a flow for the essay. Avoid stiff **stereotyped** introductions.

**Illustration 1**

***In Essay No. 3 on e-Governance, I have used one bulky paragraph to lead into the topic. It begins with a backdrop and by the closing sentence, I have managed to hit the topic.***

Ever wondered what if the spark generated by striking flint stones had not triggered a series of **cascading thoughts** in the minds of the early man? What if the rolling ability of wheel had failed to charge his grey cells?

If wheel and fire were not put to application, the utility of these tools would have remained inert and evolution story might have taken a different turn altogether. In the application of tools, borne out of human craft and intelligence, lies the key for the continuous process of growth and progress.

New paradigms open up with unimagined prospects with the process of adapting to newer tools. Inventions are able to justify their utility for the mankind by unfolding the ease with which they mingle into human lives to simplify lifestyles. With information & communication technology displaying a wide foray of opportunities, their integration in different aspects of governance is the path to welcome the future.

**Illustration 2**

***In Essay No. 13 on "Our Future on this Planet", I have begun with a quotation followed by two small (split paragraph approach) paragraphs which lead to the topic.***

*There is mercy in every place,*
*And mercy, encouraging thought.*
*Gives even affliction a grace*

True to the sentiments expressed by the playwright, the gentle showers of earth's mercy has nourished and nurtured the human existence on this planet. Like pampered sons, we have received unidirectional blessings from nature. Unmindful of our intentions, the Mother Earth presented us with plenty to even assuage our griefs and disappointments. But our refusal to grow-up and hold the responsibility baton has tested the clock of nature.

The breach of faith is a huge setback in any relationship. Our unmindful exploitation of the natural resources has tested the generation limits of our planet. The cordial co-existence has assumed the shape of a tussle, as we debate the future of humanity on our planet.

## Body

This segment constitutes the bulk of the essay. It is the time to regularly consult the mind map sheet prepared during the plotting step. Care must be taken to organize thoughts from the plotting step into similar sized paragraphs. The fluidity of thoughts complimented by the mind maps must find reflection in words in this segment.

Every idea should develop out of the preceding idea and there should be logical connection between different ideas expressed. A mere **jumble of irrelevant ideas** does not make an essay. The sense of proportion is also necessary in writing essays as in drawing of painting. An essay giving less prominence to the main theme and undue importance to non-relevant ones will look absurd.

One strand of thought must lead to another in a logically connected fashion. Any kind of **abruptness** here will disrupt the comfort of the examiner. This fluidity in expression is achieved by some effort through practice of model essays before the examination. The nuances of presentation highlighted previously must be integrated while composing this section. Keep reading the essay topic again and again while you are done with a few paragraphs. This would curtail any major deviations from the core of the topic.

## Conclusion

Do not abruptly start winding up the essay. The buildup to conclusion must begin in the last few paragraphs. One can have the liberty to briefly revisit the ideas dealt elaborately in the body and cast them in an optimistic mould. The examiner must feel that the candidate has done justice to various aspects of the topic with a threadbare analysis. This should be re-inforced in the effective summarizing paragraphs preceding the last one. The conclusion can be spread over two paragraphs. The concluding paragraph can be bulky and in a summarizing tone.

The end should not be forced; it should be as natural as possible. It should not give the impression that the writer has been compelled to stop due to lack of time or matter but that he has reached his goal and finished saying all he wanted to say about the subject.

Always end your presentation on a positive note. Even if the topic has dominant darker shades and sordid state of affairs exists in that domain, conclusion must highlight the way ahead. It must be solution oriented. Every issue has a solution which stems from **hope, perseverance** and **determination**. Be optimistic. All is not lost even if things look gloomy. There is always light at the end of the tunnel. This attitudinal reflection must be present in the conclusion. The examiner must have optimistic and a positive take away from the essay. This feel good factor will then be translated into better marks for the candidate.

**Illustration 1**

***In Essay No. 18, (Globalisation and WTO : An Era of Neo-imperialism), I have eased into the concluding paragraph by creating a backdrop in the penultimate paragraph itself. I have re-emphasized major aspects which I had touched in the essay body and tried to finish on a positive note.***

An era of neo-imperialism may fail to dawn if the strength of nation is adequate to thwart any such design. In a profit oriented dealings of the day, genuine welfare may be a rarity. Global forces will seek profit, but to curb this need from metamorphosing into greed, the role of state is crucial. The state must remain true to its commitments towards citizen and use platforms like WTO for better gains on basis of strength of economy.

As a potential superpower, India should exude such confidence and dispel any aspersions about neo-imperialism arresting its success. A **global** approach is the call of the day, where the vision is global but approaches local. Such small steps will build capacity of the country to overcome internal challenges and resist global pressures. Globalization presents opportunities. It is like an orchard, where fruits abound and can be gathered by tiptoeing around the thorns. The vehicle of globalization should be used to create the destination of Gandhian Swaraj and ensure rise of one and all.

**Illustration 2** ***A look at how Essay No. 8 (Developing a Sporting Culture in India) concludes.***

Sports in India need a renewed focus. It is time it moves away from the last pages of newspaper, last period of schools, and last priority of parents for their child's careers and domains of last benchers of schools and colleges. It is time that sporting authorities get a revamp by inclusion of more experienced players in decision making so that they understand requirement of players threadbare. It is time we understand that thrill and pride on hearing the national anthem played when Abhinav Bindra won the gold for India requires sustained efforts, hard work and support from parents. His case was of individuals fight despite the resistance of the system. Imagine how many more Bindras India can produce if the system is supportive, procedures conducive and mindset favourable for a sporting culture to flourish.

## Essay is an Expression

This book is not the final word on the art/science of writing essays. It just suggests the **approach** and **methodology** which worked successfully for me in the field of writing for the examination and otherwise. It is a piece of my experience, which I believe could help aspirants transform their potential into success in this paper. Other strategies may work equally good or even better for some.

There is no need to remember and burden yourself with the Steps that have been mentioned. Rather, one must bring them into practice while writing mock essays during preparation. Once imbibed, these steps will guide the framework of your composition effortlessly. As they become part of your systematized approach, just let your ideas and imaginations flow.

# Part B

# Collection of Essays

# Preparing Indian Society for Global Leadership

*This essay was written by the author in the Civil Services Examination 2010 where he bagged All India Rank 5.*

## "Arise, awake and stop not till the goal is reached"

This clarion call by the visionary saint still shines with relevancy. The form of challenge may have transformed but the enormity of the task demands a similar sustained display of brilliance. Honesty of spirited efforts by every countryman can weave the social fabric to richness and quicken our strides towards global leadership. The "tryst with destiny" that began over six decades back has witnessed an eventful journey of this young democracy. Beset with a unique set of challenges, India tasted its own share of successes and failures and emerged stronger with every experience. The British rule held back the flight of this golden bird, which was destined to emerge as a global leader. India failed to assume that role then, but comes with greater sense of responsibility to claim the mantle.

In the era of growing multipolarity, the role of global leadership assumes a surreal bliss. A nation - which can inspire confidence across the globe through its values and actions, a nation - which stands tall on strong fundamentals and a nation, with rich inclusive vision for the planet will only be accepted by the global community at such position. It is the preparedness of our society which will determine our stake for global leadership.

The need to prepare for global leadership is crucial in this globalised world. Leadership strengthens the voice of nation at global platform while advocating its vision and principles. It gives a bargaining power, which is inexplicably skewed in the present setting of United Nations. A crucial element of society preparedness begins with the sense of security, one can provide to the weakest. The minorities in Indian society stand testimony to the efforts of inclusiveness as part of our nation building. Our constitutional values have been bedrock to develop a wholesome society from diverse strands of religion, caste, creed and language.

This would inspire confidence in the global citizen that India would always stand for the weakest and march him to prosperity. The preparedness on cultural front is beyond comparison. Blessed with unique and diverse skills, India presents myriad dance forms, musical instruments, handicrafts, food items and skill sets to global community. The rich Indian tradition has achieved wide global recognition with the knowledge of Vedas finding a global audience.

The strength of any society can be gauged by the status of women in the society. India took years to shed its chains of orthodoxy and continues to expand the opportunities for women. The Indian growth story has witnessed an ever increasing women work force and their contribution. The wings of freedom have reached the rural thresholds also. Empowerment of women- socially, financially and politically - has transformed the face of Indian villages. Though some inhibition and social stigma remains, the winds of change are blowing for the better.

Education has been the vehicle to deliver empowerment to women. With more girl child finding access to schools, information about opportunities has percolated to the nooks of the nation. Self-help groups have infused a new era of financial independence for millions of women. Informed about their rights, they spread the confidence across the globe in India's vision and leadership. A major landmark in our society's preparedness came with the Panchayati Raj act. The decentralised framework empowered the grassroots and brought dynamic changes in the face of society.

**"Let the winds of knowledge blow in from every corner"**

*—Rig Veda*

This ancient wisdom was given a practical manifestation by democratic decentralisation. Political empowerment of women and minorities, better utilisation of resources and inclusive planning became a reality. Though discrepancies may have crept in due to insufficient autonomy to these institutions, the aberrations will be creased out in the journey of success.

Only a strong literate society can gauge the global demands and display potential to guide the global community. Education system is continuously re-inventing itself to remain relevant and accessible to the masses. Sarva Shiksha Abhiyaan and recent RTE Act can go a long way in building an educated nation with each individual enabled to achieve his potential. More coordination, however, is required between the skill set imparted and demands of the industries providing employment. Along with institutions of global repute like IITs, IIMs and AIIMS, India is striving to provide quality education to large student community through new central universities and engineering/medical/arts colleges. The functioning of the largest democracy of world has been the most livid and exemplary. In a short span of over six decades, India has negotiated the threats and shown resilience to infuse democracy as our biggest strength. The claims for global leadership get strengthened by acknowledgement of this fact by nations of the world. With increasing political maturity, the society may soon witness the much required police and electoral reforms, which will further aid in preparedness of society.

Social preparedness remains hollow until backed by strong foundations of economy. Having weathered the recent global economic downturn in a relatively unscathed manner, Indian economy has displayed its strong fundamentals and strength of financial institutions. Better proliferation of bank branches to rural India will further augment the financial inclusion essential to build a global leader. Growth must percolate to the grassroots and yield fruits of development in the form of employment and better living conditions. This has been an arena of concern, though a proactive government intervention may soon clear the logjam.

Social preparedness will remain incomplete till India manages to ensure stability and security for upcoming generations. An evergreen revolution in agriculture is the need of the hour. Food and nutritional security are sine qua non for a nation to assume global leadership. Still swathes of the nation reels under poverty, malnutrition and hunger. Focus on increasing productivity, diversification of agricultural products and timely access to credit for farmers need to be pursued on war footing to strengthen the spine of an aspiring global leader. The pace of development may have been tardy for India, but it had its own set of limitations to deal with. Huge population, poverty, extremism and religious intolerance have raise challenges for the governments of the day. With increasing developmental pace colliding with the rights of tribal communities, newer set of challenges regarding land acquisition have posed a new conundrum.

Global leader is also expected to display efficiency in tackling its own problems with solutions that inspires generations. Left wing extremism is plaguing wide domains of nation and insurgency continue to unsettle the tranquillity of north east. The achievement of critical balance of judicious use of force and developmental activities will display soundness of our policies. Balanced and inclusive development of society has to be materialised as a success story. The evolving Indian society has taken positive strides on the right path. The cancerous growth of corruption must be weeded out through legislation and change of mindsets.

The demographic dividend should be moulded to channelize the raw energy generated. The journey has left imprints in form of positive learning, which reinforces the progressive spirit of the nation. It is the strength of our society, which has propelled us as champions of the causes of developing world. The continuous preparation of society has bolstered our global image. Freedom of press and respect for human right has been established as Indian democracies shining armours. Our close competitor for global leadership, our neighbour fails to uphold these values based on tolerance and freedom of speech in the society.

A Global leader must be able to convince the nations of its vision and direction. Gandhian values of truth and non-violence were demonstrated to be the most potent weapon bringing the downfall of the Raj on the Indian soil. The technical brilliance of our manpower has been globally acknowledged as the nerve centre of major multinationals are being powered by Indian grey cells. The solutions advocated by India to major world problems emerge as a result of a pragmatic, balanced and inclusive approach, thereby appealing to the majority of the globe.

India has long suffered the scourge of terrorism but never initiated a destruction guaranteed approach of violent use of force. We never advocated violence as a solution and though apparently slow, our approach of dialogues and talks is the only means to obtain most sustaining results. India never believed in planting democracies and spoiling our shoes in the process. Rather, we have facilitated nation building and rehabilitation efforts round the globe. Our principles of Panchsheel and other foreign policy initiatives have garnered global recognition from time-to-time.

Another global catastrophe unfolding in front of our eyes is the global warming, for which pragmatic solutions have emerged from India. With an intensive focus on promotion of green energy, we display our commitments through action based programs like the green India mission. The emerging multipolarity receives a setback when the military might of nations is put on weighing scales. United States of America is miles ahead of the rest of the world on this front. But can this be a ticket to sustain the leadership role? The soft power of India has managed to encompass the world in unparalleled dimensions. Simultaneously, a scientific temper is gaining grounds in the Indian society. With more focus on research and development in coming years, the potential of rapid scientific advancements is waiting to unfold. Better equipped forces will boost the morale of each citizen of this nation.

The arena of energy security is also finding an ecological and innovative approach from the Indian land. With new researches and investments in tapping renewable sources of energy, our society is preparing for a cleaner and greener future.

**"Only when waves fall on shore, do we hear rumbling sound. Only when leaves shake the woods, do we hear rustling of the leaves."**

The preparedness of society is a journey, not a mere destination. It is a process which is geared on the energies of individuals. A process that brews on elemental successes and thrives on the spirit of excellence. With an increasingly dynamic and vibrant civil society to steer the boat through the sea of incessant storm, India should have no fear of surmounting the pinnacle. Effective tackling of social evils of society and demands of progressive legislations will help liberate us to a free uninhibited flight of potential. Permeation of education and building of a knowledge society are the stepping stones to create a nation of unlimited opportunities. Consolidating every aspect of the society by gearing them towards perfection and integrating their energies will make the global community sit up, notice and crown an able leader, worthy of being emulated.

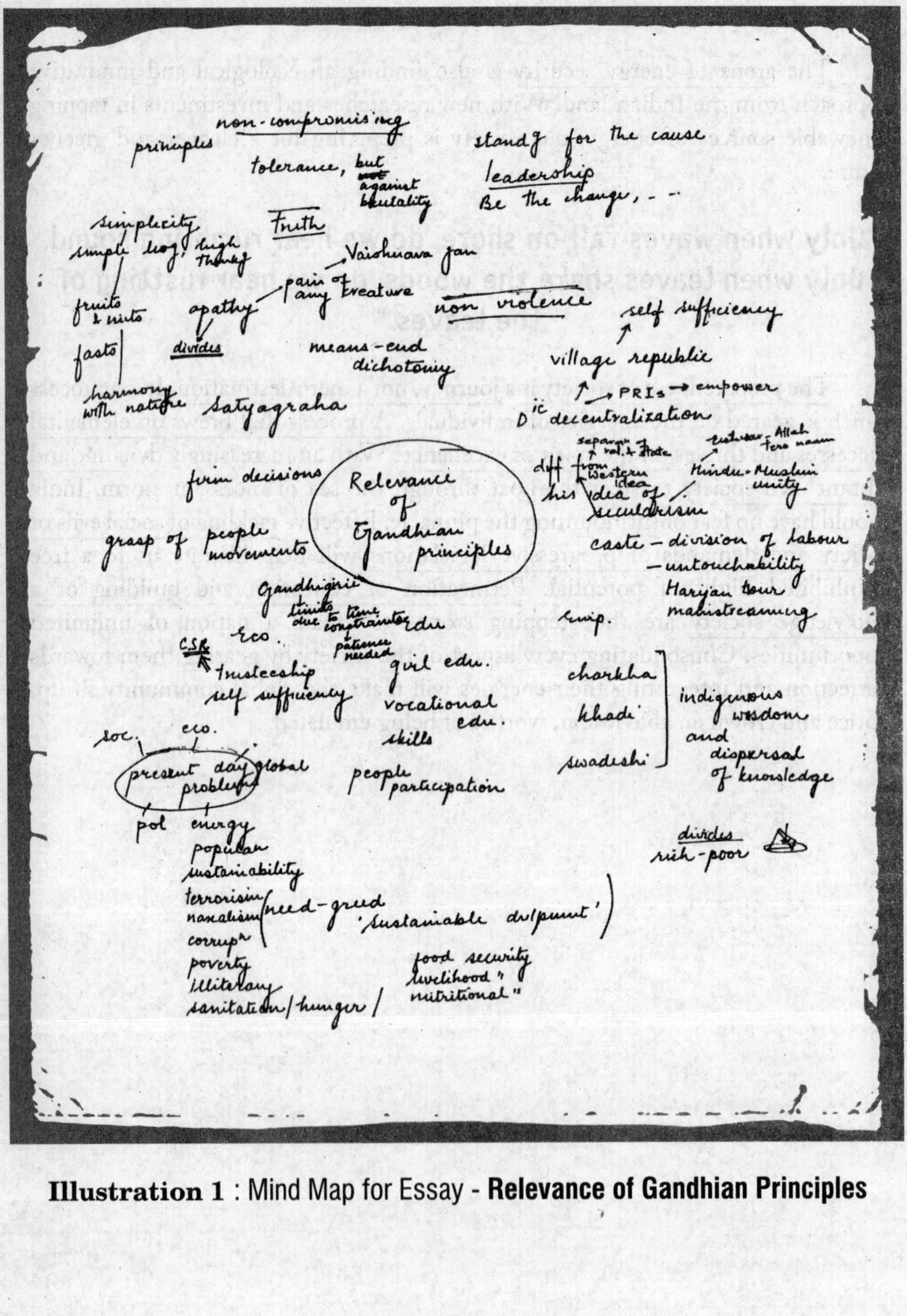


**Illustration 1** : Mind Map for Essay - **Relevance of Gandhian Principles**

# Relevance of Gandhian Principles

The human society is fast changing. With rapid developments in scientific knowledge and wider information at our disposal, the quality of life for every individual is expected to get better. Sadly, we still struggle with innumerable problems at social, economical, cultural and political levels. As the global efforts struggle to achieve the Millennium Development Goals, India has a single point of reference to solve its plethora of problems - the father of our Nation.

Even as years roll by, the Gandhian principles remain evergreen and hold power to enlighten the entire world. His simple life, rich values and enriching wisdom made him uproot the mighty British Empire. On pillars of truth and non-violence, he offers solutions, through his different principles, on issues of society, economy, politics and human substance.

## 'An eye for an eye makes the whole world blind'.

Gandhiji built his movement of Satyagraha on value premises of truth and non-violence. These proved to be the biggest arsenal to annihilate the empire. The use of brutal force on peaceful and unrelenting non-violent masses exposed the brutality and insensitivity of Britishers. The methodology appealed to the conscience. It is based on assumption of basic goodness of humanity.

In a nuclear armed world of tanks and missiles, the relevance of these values can still not be questioned. They still form the tenants of Indian foreign policy and their reflection is found in our "no-first use" clause in nuclear arena. India believes in remaining prepared as the security challenges accumulate, but aggression fails to find support in our strategies in global interactions. Even on personal level, being truthful is the most satisfying experience for a conscience driven person and also ends up as most rewarding in the long run. 'Satyamev Jayate' was vindicated when tricolor unfurled in 1947 and brought a new dawn for the nation.

Gandhian Satyagraha proved effective not only due to ideology, but also due to their timings. Gandhiji had a knack of sensing the mood of the nation. This connection to the masses emerged from his genuine concern to the pain of every individual - labour, farmer, worker and students. In the present day society, apathy has become the biggest curse. We are losing sensitivity for fellow human beings by enveloping ourselves in tight schedules and work pressures.

This sensitivity in Gandhian philosophy is for all living creatures. On his farms, he would himself attend to injured sheep or goat, even while busy with larger national issues. Humanity can offer no excuses for waiting. The world community must learn this simple Gandhian lesson to fight multiple problems of society. With little efforts and sympathy, we can improve lives of animals and people around us, by understanding the "peer parai" and rising to the occasion.

His successful mass-movements soon elevated him as the most followed mass-leader. Inspite of his popularity, he remained grounded. 'Simple living and high thinking' was the adage he lived by, undertaking rigorous fasts and largely depending on fruits and nuts; he exemplified the way of living in harmony with nature. He believed in mother earth's capacity but cautioned, "Earth has enough for everyone's needs, but not for their greed.'

As the human society faces limits from a depleting quality and quantity of resources, 'sustainable development' has become the key mantra for rectifying our deeds. At the core of this concept is the Gandhian philosophy of 'needs-based' approach. The contemporary problems of food security with depleting soil quality and conservation of biodiversity could have been avoided had we followed the wisdom of Mahatma.

As a leader, Gandhiji respected everyone's views, but made firm decisions based on his vision. He advocated the basic philosophy of "Be the change that you want to see", which continues to guide the present day civil society. His message underlines a simple philosophy of valuing every individual and his efforts. This is where the global discourse of development has failed miserably. By advocating homogeneous prescriptions for growth and implanting models irrespective of ecological diversities, problems in every society have increased manifold.

Sanitation, security, literacy or infrastructural development - all demand utilization of indigenous wisdom and traditional home grown solutions. Gandhiji valued the wisdom at grassroots and encouraged empowerment of the weakest. His idea of 'village republics' grows from this belief of cultivating self-sufficient villages through democratic decentralization.

Though Gandhian idea has been given shape in form of institutionalized Panchayati Raj Institutions, they still lack vibrancy. Only political will and informed citizens can make the Panchayati Raj, a successful model to bring development and provide solutions to disabilities of the rural masses. Though fast urbanizing, it is growth of rural India which still defines growth of our nation.

The Indian growth story is also marked by huge disparities, which are further accentuated by casteism and communalism, rearing along them hatred and divisiveness. Gandhiji had stuck at the very base of this divisive phenomenon by defining it by its genesis. He defended the castes, as a means to bring about division of labour and thereby efficiency in the society. It is our attitude of not honoring and respecting every work that accentuated the divisions to levels of untouchability.

Caste divisions have grown over time and have grown over time and have assumed virulent forms with 'honour killings' and 'mass-murders', forgetting the noble genesis explained by Mahatma.

## "Eshwar - Allah tero naam Sabko sanmati de bhagwan"

The favorite bhajan of Mahatma unfolds yet another simple wisdom which he believed in. A strong rotary of Hindu-Muslim Unity, his idea of secularism was built on respect for everyone's individual choice. The communal riots, which occasionally rear their head to disturb the fabric of society, only grow on ignorance and parochial issues.

Gandhiji is all the more relevant today when the problems in the society have assumed larger dimensions. In his stress on 'Charkha-Khadi' lay the simple strength of promoting indigenous industries and skills. In a globalized world, as we improve our intensity of trade, a large segment of our population continues to struggle with poverty and unemployment.

The promotion of vocational skills and converting them into self employment means is the sustainable means of driving out people from grasp of poverty. The spirit of 'swadeshi' should be re-ignited whereby it can coexist with the cnallenges from multi-national firms. With help of microfinance, more clusters of indigenous items should be promoted as small and cottage industries. Along with employment opportunities in villages, factories should imbibe the 'trustee ship' concept of Gandhiji by ensuring proper social security for employees. Their growing role in societal concerns should inspire them to take up causes and fulfill their corporate social responsibilities.

As every segment of the society marches forth to build an inclusive India, the contribution by women should show widening possibilities. With the women reservation bill becoming a reality, a significant step towards empowering the women has been taken. The effects should percolate to grassroots by ensuring education for the girl child. The Gandhian principle of education gave prime importance to the girl-child, as an educated girl spreads the affectivity of her education in multiple ways.

The simple life of the Mahatma advocates principles, each of which is heavy with profound wisdom. They may appear trivial and unpractical but our deviations from these basic values has been the root cause of many of our maladies. It is essential we bring back Gandhigiri in each of our lives. It will only require us to re-look and search for that basic inherent human goodness which had got buried deep down somewhere within all of us. The desire to see quick results and lack of patience due to time constraints of fast paced lives may be hurdles in evaluating these principles. But, the sustainable solution that they offer are enriching and satisfying. Similarly, even at policy level, a re-look at basic Gandhian philosophies may re-orient our efforts to bring inclusive growth and happiness to the faces of millions.

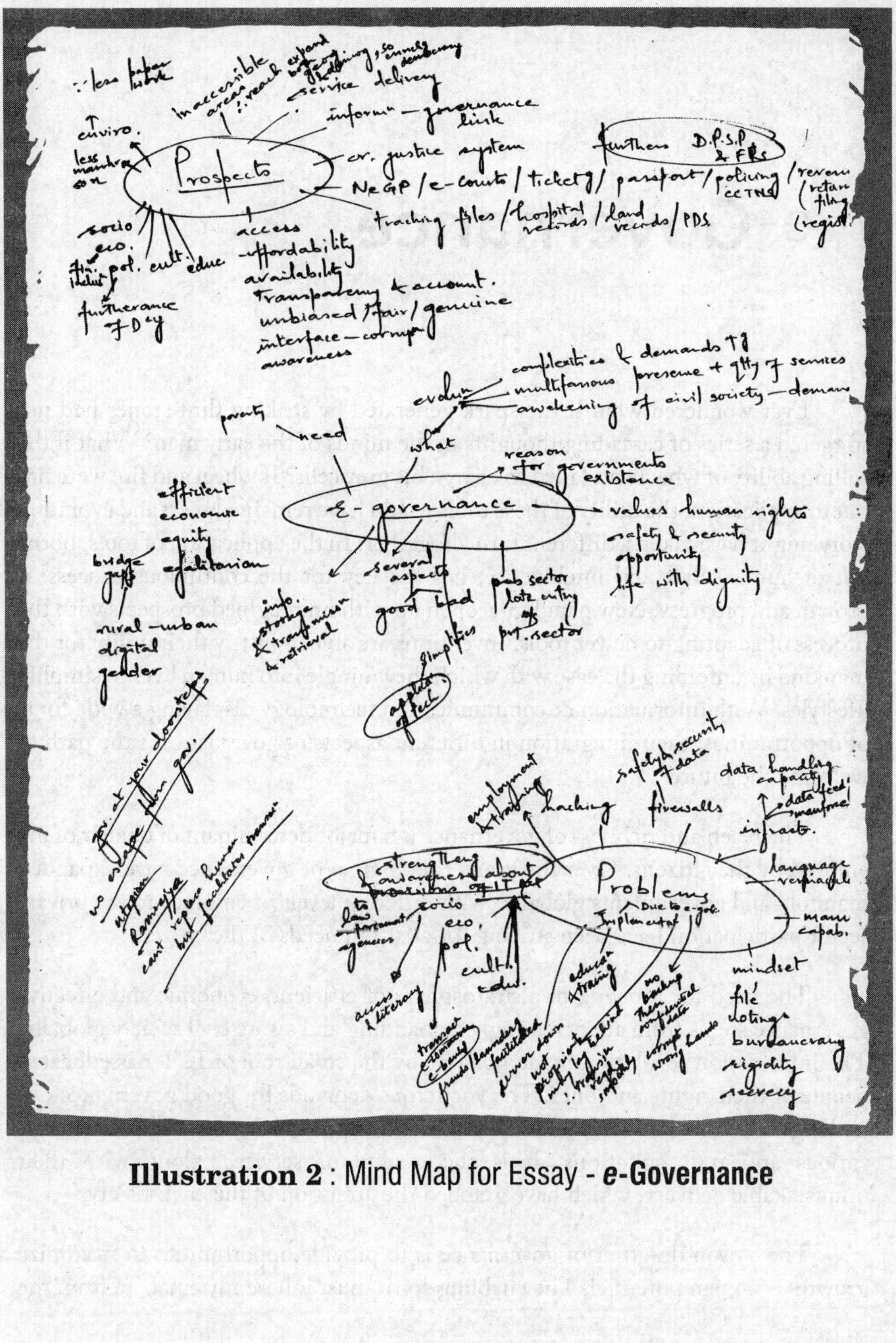


**Illustration 2** : Mind Map for Essay - ***e*-Governance**

# e-Governance

Ever wondered what if the spark generated by striking flint stones had not triggered a series of cascading thoughts in the minds of the early man? What if the rolling ability of wheel had failed to charge his grey cells? If wheel and fire were not put to application, the utility of these tools would have remained inert and evolution story might have taken a different turn altogether. In the application of tools, borne out of human craft and intelligence, lies the key for the continuous process of growth and progress. New paradigms open up with unimagined prospects with the process of adapting to newer tools. Inventions are able to justify their utility for the mankind by unfolding the ease with which they mingle into human lives to simplify lifestyles. With information & communication technology displaying a wide foray of opportunities, their integration in different aspects of governance is the path to welcome the future.

The reach and richness of governance is a major determinant of quality of life enjoyed by the citizens. Over the years, the domain of governance have expanded manifold and governments globally- with different levels of embrace to the private sector participation have been striving to satisfy all needs of the citizens.

The need for evolving to a stratosphere of efficient, economic and effective governance stems from an increasingly demanding and aware civil society globally. The information revolution made possible by the small tool of ICT has educated people of their rights and dues. The vociferous demands for good governance can no longer be muted. It broke out in form of Arab spring this year or closer home as various anti-graft agitations. It is the quality of services, along with their unmistakable delivery, which have grabbed the attention of the civil society.

The [illegible]ason de-attier of governance is to provide opportunities to maximize growth [illegible]nan potential. The enabling spirit must inherently emanate from the core of any governance. It carries immense trust and expectations of the masses and must imbibe all 'goodness' for its' longevity. The path for dawn of good governance has been simplified by tools presented by advancements in Information and Communication Technology. The adaptation of these tools in different domains of governance has potential to unleash an era of e-governance. With varying degrees of progress, nations across the globe have progressed on absorbing the tools of ICT to make their governance economic, efficient and effective.

Simplification of processes and ease of storage, transmission and retrieval of information lie at the heart of transformative process of governance using ICT. Web-enabled service delivery, advanced tip of the finger communication facilities and increasing ease in handling large volumes of data have found varying utility to bring smiles on millions of faces.

e-governance brings governance to the doorsteps of the individual. With an ingrained tenet of non-discrimination, it manages to drive systems to provide an equitous environment. The gulfs of class, color, language, region or religion fail to impede the service delivery. Every citizen who meets the defined norms and criterion stands eligible to receive benefits, escaping the judgmental prejudices linked with human involvement.

Another prospect which can mark its presence in governance with increasing absorption of ICT is accessibility. Several inhibitions cloud the mind space of individual while approaching any government office. Often improper knowledge about nuances of schemes or eligibility criteria or procedural requirements prevents a person from approaching the facility provided by the policy. The maze of counters and desks induce high degree of repulsion, esp. in population from rural or disadvantaged background. The implementation efficiency of the policy gains a boost by ease of its access through tools of e-governance in form of interactive screens in enabling kiosks.

With wider diffusion of e-governance, a daily labor will not have to forgo his wage for one day for an unsuccessful trip to the revenue office. On the other end of the spectrum, a multimillionaire will be facilitated through informational portal for avenues of investment. He can browse about opportunities, transfer amounts online and obtain single window clearances for his project without encountering hassles of red-tapism.

Government transactions have been marked by veils of secrecy. The winds of change have begun by the RTI legislation. They are bound to intensify with adoption of e-governance at different levels of stakeholders' interface with the system. With computerization creeping in at all levels of governance, file movement tracking can become simpler and accountability ascertained. Deadlines, for clearance or decision making, can be accurately monitored by the complainant himself through web-enabled access.

An era of e-governance will help in curbing generation of black money and emergence of a parallel economy. As the interface between the service provider and consumer becomes electronic in nature, discretion of individuals will be diminished and activities of middlemen removed from the chain. Citizens will be entitled to obtain value for their money. With their actions under an electronic scanner, transparency will stifle out corruption and drive in professionalism in manner of operation of government officials. This will have direct impact on efficiency and effectiveness of the systems with increasing productivity contributing to a healthier economy.

With proliferation of banking and e-transaction facility, leakages from the government schemes can be plugged. Smart cards enabled cash transfer directly to the account of the worker will widen and strengthen the social security net. Tools of e-governance can revolutionize the efficacy of already prevalent government schemes. Benchmarks of efficiency using e-governance in PDS have been set by the Chattisgarh Government. Success stories of cash transfer in NREGA have also highlighted the enormous potential held by e-governance.

Along with strengthening, financial inclusion and lifting the masses above the poverty line, e-governance provides the perfect solution for dissemination of information. Village resource centres have become a reality, advising farmers about the suitable crop, cropping pattern, fertilizers and pesticides to be used. Experts from different regions can collaborate their rich experiences cutting down the barriers of geographical distances and enrich the poor and needy with timely advices.

Similarly, health services have received a major boost with constraints of inaccessibility and poverty failing to be an impediment in getting world class treatment. Web cams and tele-conferencing tools have shrunk the distances and brought patients closer to their saviors.

Another arena of good governance is delivery of value in form of education. e-governance steps in to connect universities and facilitate seamless exchange of information. e-governance can soon help in making the knowledge society a reality. Students sitting in different corners of this nation benefit simultaneously as they attend to nuances of nanotechnology or molecular kinematics from the experts, sitting in their comfort.

e-governance has potential to transfer the entire culture of governing and those governed. It expands the horizon of opportunities available for any citizen cutting across narrow barriers of caste, colour, language or religion. It furthers the noble ambitions the framers of our constitution by facilitating the spirit of fundamental rights and directive principles of state policy. The tools of e-governance add dignity to the lives of individuals- the poor, marginalized and struggling with some or other deficit afflicting their lives.

e-governance will also bring about an environment friendly ecological governance framework which will reduce the huge amount of paper requirement to carry out the government proceedings. It will, thereby, contribute to nurturing of a greener and cleaner planet.

As the largest employer of masses, the government machinery ensures livelihood for millions at different levels. With different amount of skills required to carry out their duties, several employees lack in even the elementary knowledge of computers. To unfold an era of e-governance, a massive training programme carried with the help of experts and universities a pre-requisite. Another implementation hazard is the infrastructural sufficiency desired to promote the tools of e-governance in every nook and corner of the nation. An interconnected network of communicating devices at block, district, state and central level with suitable timely upgrades will be essential as the backbone of e-governance paradigm. Sufficient speed of processing and bandwidth for data transfer pose challenge for bringing about e-governance in full measure.

Another problem in implementation of e-governance is in form of safety and security of huge amount of data involved. Any government department caters to needs of millions of citizens and thereby has to deal with substantial amount of data- much of which may be confidential in nature. Hacking and data piracy need to be guarded against by taking suitable preventive measures. These have to be dynamic and must evolve continuously to tackle the evil designs of hackers. The NIC will have to be equipped to emerge as the hub of proficiency to ensure data safety. Firewalls and latest anti-virus updates must be developed and made available at all centres.

With a huge linguistic diversity within the stretch of nation, blanket software dissemination may fail to yield results at the grassroots. Entrepreneurship must be promoted vigorously to come up with vernacular solutions for the interactive features of e-governance equipments. Rural India will benefit from the technology only when it is redesigned to their comfort levels. More emphasis on sight and sound features will enhance their utility for the millions still enveloped in darkness of illiteracy.

Living in an era of uncertainties, e-governance presents risk in form of survival of data. The problem stares in form of back-up requirement of data being handled electronically. Certain fields of sensitive nature may not be worth gambling upon and a back up paper record will have to be kept till an adequate reliability and faith is generated about handling of data.

The transformation from a paper and file based governance to an electronically advanced is a journey every nation undertakes. Preparedness is a continuous process of refinement of available technology, its' customization, absorption in government systems and societies' preparation to utilize it with ease. At our stage of journey, we still encounter slow servers, irregular data download speeds, incidents of phising, hacking and frauds, and regular unsatisfactory grudges linked to e-banking and e-commerce. These and several other irregularities still need ironing. The awareness about features if IT Act amongst the public and also among the law enforcement agencies must be increased. Simultaneously, the provisions of this Act must be periodically reviewed and strengthened to meet the emerging challenges.

The biggest impediment, however, stems from the human element. The lack of will to adapt and inertia to continue in the regime of secrecy and paperwork stall any progress to bring about all colours of e-governance. As a developing nation, battling with myriad unique problems, e-governance sounded a distant dream. However, steps have been taken on the path to materialize this dream. Railway ticketing and passport registration led by example to ensure hassle free service to the citizens. Though some snags have been observed with server failure for tatkaal booking, the railways need to rise to the occasion and display its' commitment of service through electronic means.

Similarly, the e-court programme is another ambitious project which has potential to change the face of the judicial system of the nation. As a critical component of governance, the judiciary is overburdened and delays plague the delivery of justice. The e-court project will link the courts and facilitate sharing of judgments, transmission of date and tracking the status of the cases.

A similar movement is brewing with the CCTNS in the police department - a wing responsible for main-taining law and order by active crime prevention and detection. Linking of police stations with HQ and beats, real time monitoring of criminal activities, electronic data and fingerprint recording and sharing can go a long way in developing an efficient and proactive policing unit, which inspires confidence and faith in public. The NeGP is yet another drive to smoothen the movement of files across departments. Revenue departments have also displayed flair in facilitating the assessee by employing e-tools for filing of registration and returns. Similar efforts by several states in land registration can go a long way in solving major disputes in the rural heartland of the nation.

In different field, introduction of elements of computerization has helped in easing and simplifying processes and improving service delivery to the stakeholders. e-governance measures in offices help in streamlining complex procedures, enhancing efficiency and cutting down the red tapism linked delays. The application of e-governance is still in the nascent stages in the developing Indian society and the limitless possibilities it has in its fold are tough to even imagine. As its introduction will strike on the selfish interests of several groups, there are big lobbies resisting its application in different governance related programs and procedures. The challenge for government and bureaucracy lies in driving its percolation to the grassroots, in spite of such resistance. e-Governance is the way forward for bringing an era of transparent, accountable, responsive, effective, efficient and economical governance. It is a tool which has the potential to simplify procedures, practices and alter service delivery in a radical manner. There is nothing which can deny its' arrival on the scene. The pace of its adoption will soon become a determining factor in anointment of our nation as global superpower.

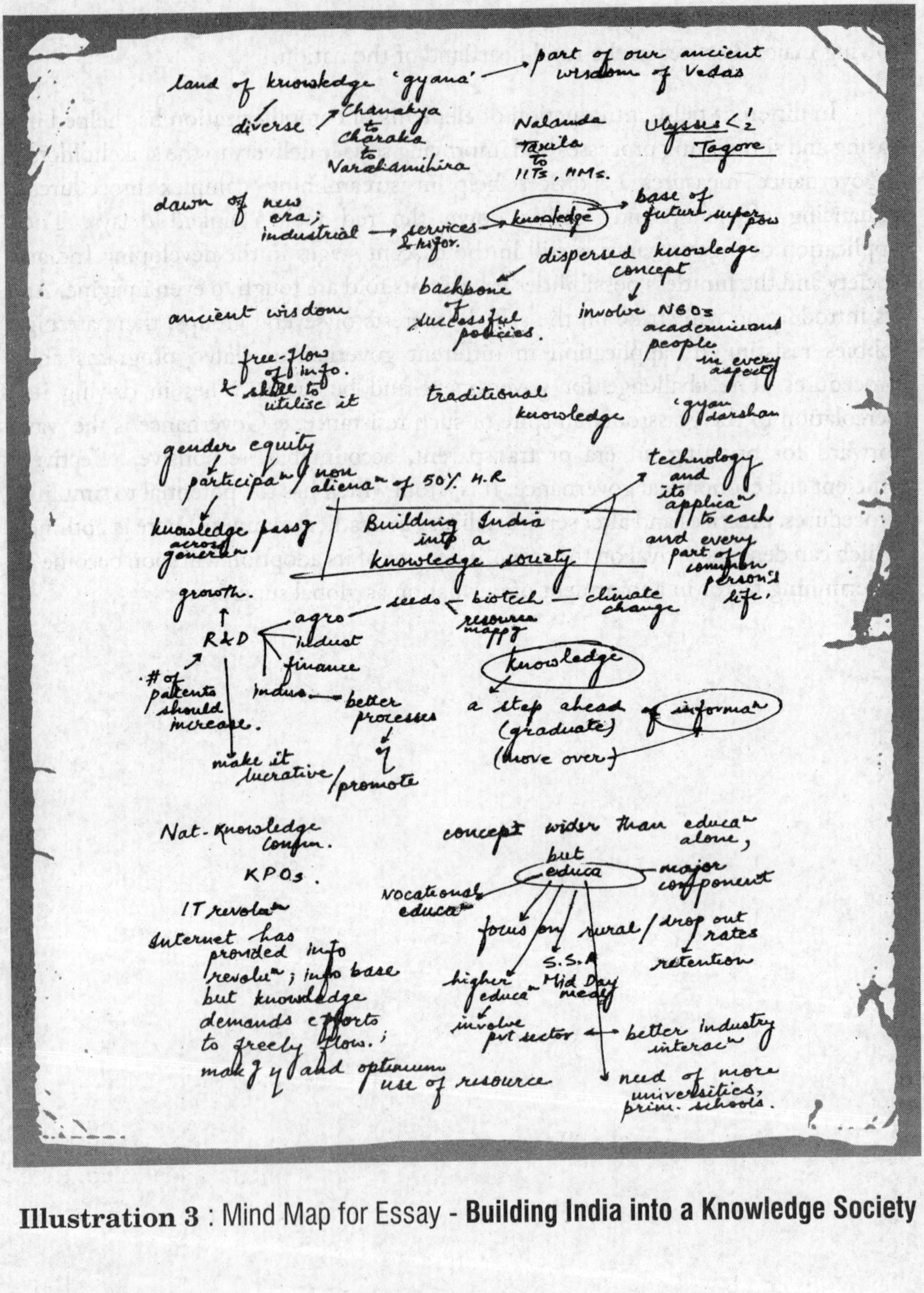


**Illustration 3** : Mind Map for Essay - **Building India into a Knowledge Society**

# Building India into
# A Knowledge Society

**"Yet, all knowledge is an archway, whose margin fades for ever and ever"**

The poet felt helpless, yet enriched as he chased a dream; a dream of conquering knowledge, the very pursuit of which was enriching his life each passing moment. Such is the power of knowledge.

As a tool to broaden one's vision and mental horizon, to introduce one to galaxy of unexplored avenues and opportunities and to 'empower' human existence - the key lies in developing and nurturing knowledge based society – a concept from which we deviated in the path of our development – needs to be rekindled and re-ignited. Our tradition and culture have developed on strong bedrock of knowledge. The town planning and social management schemes of the Indus Valley Civilization bear testimony to this fact.

The 'quest for gyana' forms the spirit of our ancient wis m highlighted in Vedas and other scriptures. The multi faceted dimension of 'knowledge' find reflection through prism of diversity in form of Charaka, Varahamchira, Chanakya, Patanjali – each an embodiment of pinnacle of knowledge in his own field.

From being the global cynosure for knowledge through rich religions and their teachings to a need for revival has been a long Indian Saga. Grappling with problems of agrarian crisis, health, infrastructure, inequity and symptoms of unplanned overgrowth, the refuge can only be sought in bringing about a holistic solution. Our schemes and plans have suffered from segmental and sectoral outlooks. With a vision to create a 'knowledge society' both planning and its implementation will receive a fresh look.

The concept of knowledge graduates a step ahead of information. IT Revolution ushered us into an age of connectivity and availability of information at ease. However, information without ability of its application serves little purpose. This transformation will bring about dynamic changes in every aspect of the society, no sooner we bring about the percolation of knowledge to every aspect of human life, right at the grassroots.

Agriculture drives the wheels of our economy and the stagnation in productivity stands as a roadblock, as indentified in the Approach paper for the XIth Plan. A revolution is eagerly anticipated. Though mechanisms exist, application is suffering. The extension services can play a vital role through E-kiosks or village resource centres or NGO organized researchers - farmers meet where region and crop specific advice, advancements in technology, better farm practices could be directly passed on to the farmers.

Agricultural universities and research institutions will have to assume the leadership in laying foundations for this knowledge society. Better application of biotechnology to develop transgenic crops can save farmers from vagaries of nature. This aspect has gained more significance in the face of climate changes occurring through global warming and a need for better preparedness in food security is paramount.

## 'Ideas fuel the engines of innovation.'

The significance of cultivating and encouraging ideas should be appreciated. In this quest, a reform is desired in the outlook of the society, which in turn should find reflection in our education system. Knowledge, as a holistic concept, goes beyond education. Yet, education can provide a strong pillar for the edifice.

Our education planning demands a dual approach to meet the challenges of building a knowledge society. The linear approach calls for building more colleges and universities to streamline the skewed proportion with population. As suggested by the National Knowledge Commission, extension to rural segments needs further strengthening. Schemes like Sarva Shiksha Abhiyan and Mid-Day Meal should be followed vigorously to arrest the drop-out rate and achieve universalization of primary and elementary education.

On the 'non-linear' front, the mere addition of more schools and colleges will not solve the problem in a sustainable manner. We could prepare a brigade of 'literates' not 'educated' unless the attention shifts on quality of education. This is where strength and capacity of private sector needs to be harnessed, especially in the field of higher education. With better links to industries, they are equipped to understand the skills and requirements of the enterprises and could incorporate those as a part of a dynamic curriculum.

Initiatives like industry student interaction would enhance better flow of knowledge and shrink the barriers. More ITIs and skill improvement centres in rural areas can empower individuals and make them 'discover' the 'rationale' of education.

From an era of "services driven growth", the economy is also on a look out for a stable, self sustaining, assured growth pattern. Knowledge fuels growth by encouraging research, whereby a virtuous growth cycle can be established through asset creation and generating employment. Steps to improve our patenting regime and making research avenues more lucrative would be a positive step in right direction.

'Knowledge society' is an empowering arena, which seeks to bridge gulfs and provide each human a chance to develop his potential by removing boundaries from availability of avenues. It turns out to be a spark to bring vibrancy in the society. It refers not only to technical knowledge, but also about rights and grievance redressal mechanisms.

It strengthens the bedrock of parliamentary democracy as it recognizes the 'power of one'. It empowers the marginalized to question the reasons behind his poverty and provides him with opportunities to come out of it. It arms the citizens with Right to Information (RTI) and demand responsibility, driving in transparent efficient and participative governance.

In our efforts to bring about such 'knowledge revolution', Gandhian wisdom should serve as a guiding philosophy. He emphasized on knowledge residing at the grassroots and need for its logical implementation. This simple recognition of valuing our traditional wisdom and dispersed knowledge could drive away number of problems facing our society.

People's participation and contribution will promote free flow of knowledge to bring about indigenous solutions. Issues of climate threat, resource depletion, efficient use of energy and even terrorism would reduce with an aware and involved citizen. Knowledge could link the society and reduce incidences of socio-economic neglect that breeds suppressive elements. It would enable a farmer to appreciate ISRO's programmes and also garner benefits from them.

In the arena of sports, knowledge would equip us with better techniques to make us globally competitive. Researches for industrial processes and devices would in turn drive in direct revenue. The commercial launching of Italian satellite recently, apart from garnering revenues, has brought global recognition. Scientific achievements elevate our global status and enhance our image of 'superpower-in-making'.

The smooth networking of knowledge can diversify avenues in rural areas. It facilitates the efforts of government to reach the people through telemedicine, e-banking and video-conferencing. Social and gender equity find their source in empowered citizenry. A better participation of women in decision making at level of family, society and nation could alter the spots of orthodoxy.

## 'Knowledge is Power'

The time is ripe to identify and apply this power to illuminate every dark corner of our nation. A networking of schools – universities - industries - farmers - customers demands intensification. A knowledge society is a blend where our traditional wisdom is synthesized with modern advancements. It is an effort which aligns growth to development of an individual, society and nation. It empowers 'aam aadmi' and enables efforts of nation-building – a nation where Tagore's vision is given a concrete from - "A nation where the head is held high and the mind is without fear."

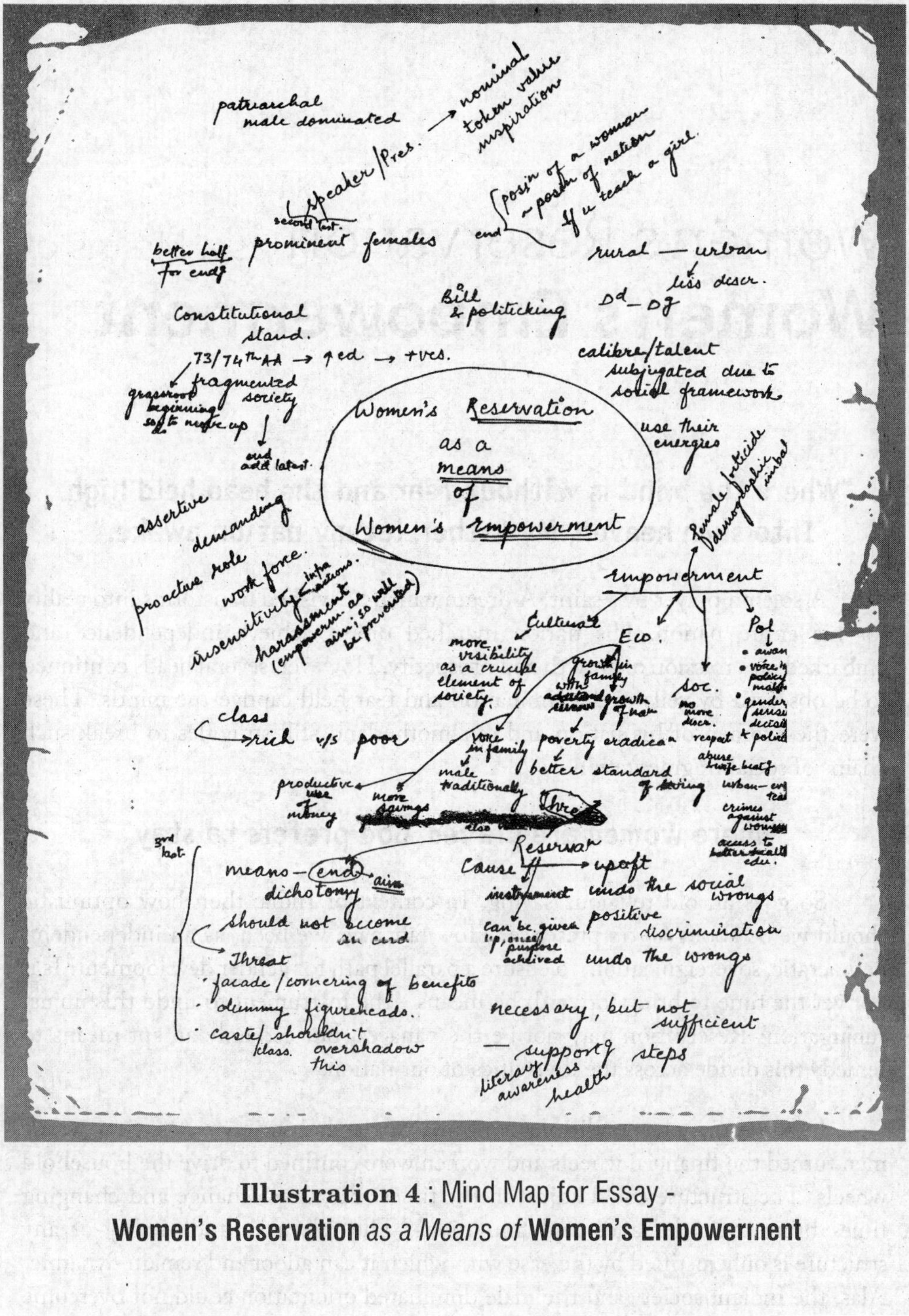


**Illustration 4** : Mind Map for Essay -
**Women's Reservation** *as a Means of* **Women's Empowerment**

# Women's Reservation as a Means of **Women's Empowerment**

**"Where the mind is without fear and the head held high. Into such heaven, My father, let my nation awake."**

A solemn prayer by a saint. A dream which he wished transforms into reality for his entire nation. His nation marched on to achieve independence and embarked on a mission of growth and prosperity. However, several heads continued to be obscured by veils of discrimination and fear held captive the minds. These were the 'women of his nation and our motherland still struggles to break such chains of social fragmentation.

**'Where women are prayed, God prefers to stay'**

So goes an old religious saying. In context of India, then how optimistic should we be about God's presence? How fair have we been, as an independent, democratic, sovereign nation, to ensure a parallel path for gender development? Is it not yet the time to bring forward the means - the instrument to undo this unjust subjugation? Reservation may not be the panacea, but certainly an apt means to remedy this divide across the diversities of our nation.

Indian society has traditionally been a patriarchal society - A society where men turned the financial wheels and women were confined to drive the household wheels. The structure could adjust in the times. But times change and changing times bring their demands and limitations. The relevance and vitality of any structure is only justified by the ease with which it can adopt and remain dynamic. Alas, the Indian, society and the male dominated orientation could not overcome the inertia with ease.

As members of the emerging economic giant, it becomes essential that both genders contribute and benefit from the growth of nation. However, women in India, continue to suffer from burden of social norms, traditions and definitions. It is an irony that globally considered as an epitome of strength, love and care women are still 'the weaker sex' in our society. Irony nevertheless, it is a shame as well.

The Constitutional frames showed acumen by inserting positive discrimination to raise the participation of women. However, the male dominated politics of generations have yielded breathing space to women, ever so slowly. A revolution of sorts was thereby achieved when the historic 73rd and 74th Amendment Act, through Reservation ensured representation of women in grass root levels of democracy.

Reservation as a tool is a means to ensure representation. It creates space. It may not be sufficient, but undoubtedly an essential step to bring forth a segment which has been socially subjugated for ages. Women reservation is a crying call of the society to empower women and make them partners in all spheres in true sense. From times of Sati and Jauhar to the need of being assertive and demanding, Indian women have seen a long journey – from an era of uplift and emancipation to the need for empowerment today. Reservation provides a solution to lend voice to women of the nation and can be removed once women achieve a position of coequals in society.

Political empowerment of women has made a modest beginning at Panchayats and Municipality level. With a recent increase in reservation to half, women will achieve a better say in policy making and implementation. However, party politicking at the national level has not yet allowed the Women Reservation Bill to see the light of the day. Different theories are floated for its' opposition. While some argue that reservation should be on basis of constituency, others demand reservation in ticket distribution by the parties. The logjam has stupefied the voice of women, in the process.

Political empowerment will radiate gender sensitiveness in policies and increase in awareness about rights at the grass root. Women's needs, problems and issues will be highlighted in forums and discussions, only when women in sufficient numbers manage to reach such forums. Reservation will provide the initial thrust to overcome the social barrier and resistance. Reservation in major employment schemes and in political bodies will enhance the earning capacity of households. Economic empowerment of women could drive houses away from evil grip of poverty on a sustainable basis. As a contributor, to the better standard of living of the family, the lady can then hold her head high.

Economic empowerment also provides a shield against ill treatment and abuse that women in both rural and urban India have grown habitual to. As an earning member, capable of sustaining herself, she will break the threads of traditional dependence on the male. On equal footing she can demand her rights, assert herself and be recognized. Several women in urban India have witnessed such empowerment in recent decades and reservation could further add to this growing strength in number.

The ability of the women to plan judiciously and run the house hold is recognized globally. The self help group (SHG) movement also relies on the uprightness of women and this judicious use for saving and productive purposes will enhance when they earn their own money. Reservation will compulsorily bring out women from their households to explore avenues of growth and utilization of their skills. A huge reserve of talent has been untapped. A skillful segment has remained untouched from being part of workforce of this nation. Reservation will help in aligning these energies for the progress of nation.

Empowered women will enrich the civil society of the nation and will drive the virtuous cycle to work for more disadvantaged lot. This social empowerment will help them take proactive part in aligning some distortions of the society. Women will then find a voice against eve-teasing and insensitivity in urban areas. They can better handle the crusade against female foeticide and thereby rectify the demographic imbalance.

Reservation in forces would not only tap talent of women in combat skills, but also generate healthy competition in male dominated arenas. This will auger well for sensitivity of forces - an account of constant criticism in recent past. More gynecologists, specialists and medical practitioners will truly drive in a fair distribution of human resource of the nation.

The aim to bring in reservation is to enthuse dynamism in Indian society. By active participation of women; nation building will be smoother, equitous and more rapid. Reservation, however, should remain the vehicle and not the destination. The caution, in exercising this approach lies in protecting against usurping of this vehicle. In name of women representation, dummy figureheads are threats, which can derail the affectivity of this means. Male counterparts actively wielding power, in name of elected wives, have spoiled the spirit in several areas.

Another concern, due to inherent stratifications of Indian social mosaic is the cornering of benefits by influential, rich and dominant. It is here that other supplementary and equally crucial elements have to step in and support reservation.

An efficient administration and high level of awareness driving people -participation should condemn and cremate such practices.

Women empowerment is a journey the Indian bandwagon has begun, though slowly and hopefully steadily, to win the race. The fight has to be fought on several fronts - but most critical is on the attitudinal front. Men must accept the strength and talent of women and provide that crucial space for harmonious existence.

With a woman as the head of state and another as the speaker of People's House, India should set an example in empowering women. Women of this nation have brought laurels and global recognition in diverse fields. Be it Kalpana Chawla or Saina Nehwal, Kiran Desai or Indira Noori, Mrs Indira Gandhi or Lata Mangeshkar - Idols galore for Indian women. The need of the times demands them to be proactive members of the changing times. They should utilize the ladder of reservation and shine beyond in all hues of their talent and enigma. The story of any nation is often judged by glancing at the standard of empowerment of its women. It is high time that governance in our nation accepts this and proactively involves the synergy from this segment. It is, thereby; time to project the 'better halves' as the 'better half' on the national level.

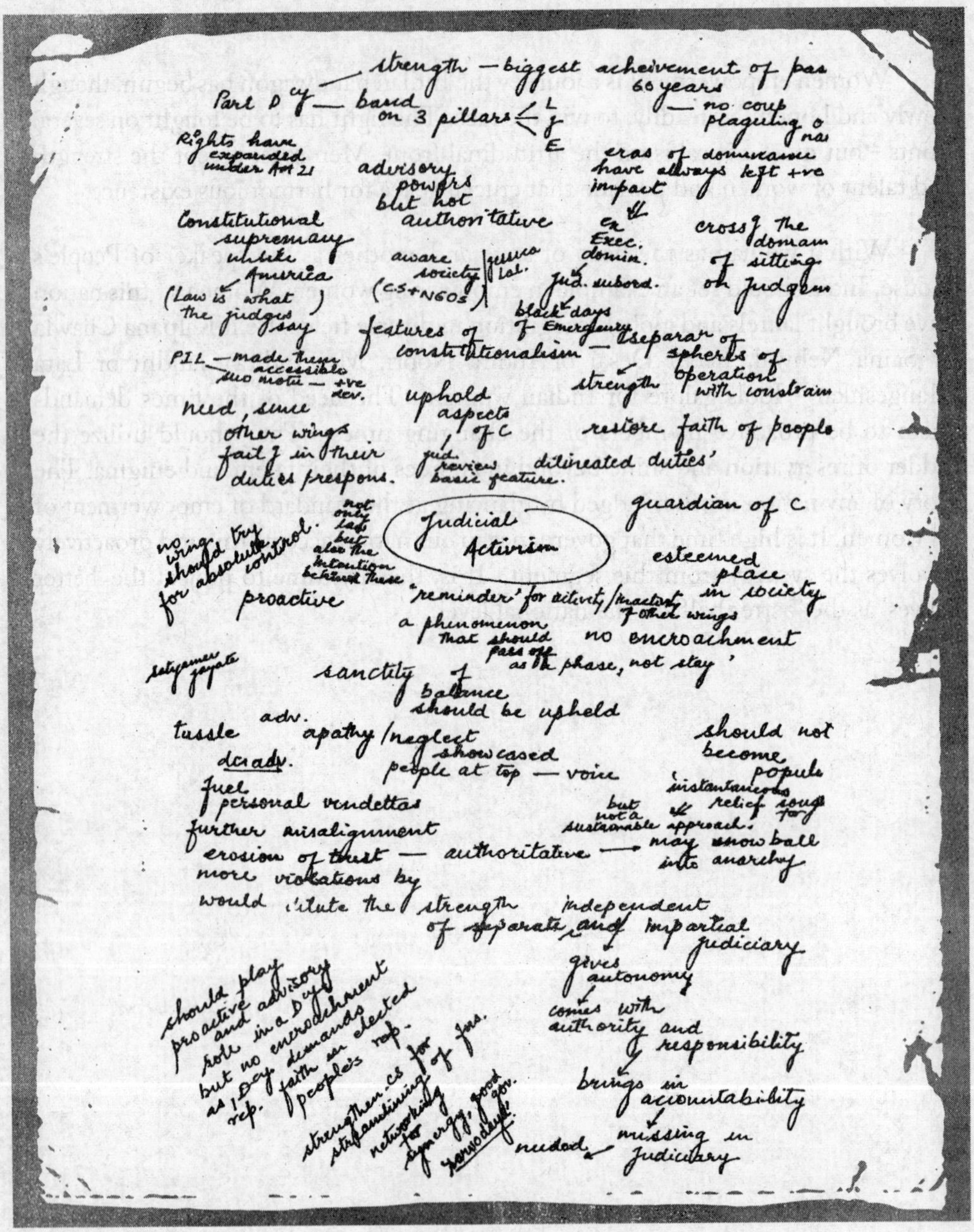


**Illustration 5** : Mind Map for Essay - **Judicial Activism**

# Judicial **Activism**

The 'tryst with destiny' that commenced for India as an independent nation, sixty years back, has travelled several chapters of struggle, toil and triumph. Amongst glaring problems in a diverse society, the vision of nation-building has marched strongly on bedrock of constitutional strength. Through setbacks and achievements, tragedies and celebrations, defeats and victories - India has emerged as a stronger nation every single time. The fine balance between three wings of parliamentary democracy have stood the test of time and justified the conviction of adopting a parliamentary democracy.

The success saga of our nation emanates from the foundational solidity imparted through constitution. The founding fathers delimited the areas of operation of the three pillars - judiciary, executive and legislature - in such a meticulous manner, which complements the efforts of each, for nation building.

Though tussle for dominance has marked various phases between these pillars, yet each such phase has enriched the functioning of our democracy. India emerged stronger after the setbacks of black days of emergency, when executive authoritarianism upset the delicate balance. In lives of dynamic nations, such event of activism occurs as a 'phase' - a period to introspect about the lacunae. The recent era of judicial activism should usher in a similar re-look and diagnosis to bring forth corrective measures.

Judiciary has always held an esteemed position in our society. As a position of dignity and faith, a judge has been the 'mai-baap' of the 'aam aadmi'. As an institution, it has provided refuge to one and all-irrespective of caste, community, color, sex, region or religion. Upholding the sacred duty of safeguarding the constitution', several landmark judicial decisions have time and again rescued the rights of the citizen from any legislative or executive excesses. However, this fine balance of operation has witnessed a deviation in certain recent issues. Judiciary, under the noble cloak of 'people's interest', has often transgressed the domains of its jurisdiction. How healthy are these trends in the life of a parliamentary democracy? Which direction should our polity evolve from here?

The quagmire further deepens as people consider judiciary as their refuge and protector against injustices. The growing depletion of faith of citizens in the state machinery is an arena of grave concern. 'Judicial Activism' is only a symptom, not a disease. It comes as a thermometer to indicate the brewing discontent amongst the citizens against a failing state. Both the legislature and the executive should view this, not mere as an encroachment of judiciary in their domains, but rather as a reminder to be sensitive, proactive and responsive to needs of people.

The era of judicial activism emerged strongly with the option of PIL. It calls for proactive citizenry - a basis to develop a vibrant civil society. Courts can also pick cases 'suo moto' in case of gross violation of human rights by any state or private machinery. Focus remains on the primacy of people's power. The concern of common man and his empowerment – social, economic and political – remain the ethos of parliamentary democracy.

Widening scope of Article 21, ensuring the right to live with dignity also adds to the responsibilities of State. Widening gulfs in the society of gender, social equity, financial merits, and digital divides highlight the herculean task faced by the state. In face of such demands, an inefficient, secretive and corruption ridden state machinery has fallen short in meeting the inclusive criteria of development.

Events like non-registering of FIRs, elitist favours, collusion amongst bureaucratic machinery to shield and propagate domination at the cost of distributive justice have necessitated the need for courts to be proactive. The sheer apathy or brutal excess of executive actions has become a norm, rather than an exception.

In such an era of demanding, assertive and aware citizens, emergence of judiciary as a stronger pillar was a natural consequence. The establishment of an independent judiciary to check the validity of legislative actions, not to violate the constitutional spirit, has been justified through its measures of checks and balances.

However, the growing concern, plaguing the ethos of a swift functioning democracy, remains about the extent of this authoritarianism. In a parliamentary democracy, voice of people finds reflection through the representatives in law making body. With limited figment of accountability, how far can the encroachment by such an institution accepted?

the traditions. It becomes a super-identity of the person, separate from his individual skills, achievements and recognitions.

These inherited patterns of thoughts and actions trace their origin to several ages back in the history of time. Any individual growing up in present times would naturally find many of them different from the other activities of his time. Each generation leaves the world as a different place than as they found it. The perceived idea of "modernity" simply arises from the fact that change is the only constant in this universe. Individuals' sensibilities are linked to the society he grows up in and in the times when the pace of change has intensified by bounds, present day norms often clash with the demands of traditions.

"Modernity" is often perceived in a negative and vulgar fashion by traditionalists. The entire present generation is generalized as "rebels" who are "corrupted" under the influence of foreign exposure. They are tarnished with "lack of gravity" in their conduct and thoughts. Traditionalists brand them as free spirited individuals without any respect for tradition and leading a shallow existence under the façade of modernity. With such popular gross generalization, the traditionalists hardly afford a chance to this generation to blend and strike "friendship" with traditions.

Home is the perfect location where friendship between tradition and modernity can seep into an individual. Most of the traditions of religions which survive till date can be traced back to our holy scriptures. They even have some or other scientific rationale mentioned therein. This fact is generally overlooked and the explanations hardly known by the ignorant elders to the querying minds. The very reason of survival of traditions has been their mass acceptance as nothing counterfeit can claim to have such survivability.

Traditions link us to our rich heritage. They involve generations into a big family bound by an intangible emotional linkage. A set of traditions go on to define the way of life - and this cultural connectedness provides a distinct flavor and identity. Every individual must be made aware of this belongingness to a fraternity, which must be a matter of pride and privilege. It is this valued belongingness which is recognized globally as the rich cultural heritage of our nation. It may not have tangible manifestations but the spiritual connectivity which blesses every soul is enlightening.

Traditions must be cherished and never forced upon an unwilling mind. The survival of traditions stands testimony to the feature of flexibility. It must grant freedom to the individual and a choice to disconnect oneself from the bigger identity it imparts. Some rituals associated with the traditions may appear time consuming and impractical to a "modern" mind. Tradition must grant space for every "modern" individual to exercise the choice of following or leaving certain rituals. Rigidity is stiffening. Rigidity breeds discontent.

Modernity is not designed as a natural friend of tradition. Beyond the perceived image of a modern individual created by traditionalists due to a different set of sensibilities of the growing up eras, lies the pragmatic individual. Modernity is reflected in an individual's outlook. A modern person will have a outlook molded by the state of society he is witnessing. His ideas have been formed in a globalized world - a world which talks of gender equality, extremism and terrorism, nuclear states, electronics and IT sophistications and bridging the class-religion divides. The variations in his thought processes from the ones which are traditionally carried over are bound to exist, but they should not become the reasons of animosity. Rather a blend of traditional wisdom and modern outlook must be aspired for to dispel the anxieties created by any clash of ideas.

A modern individual's outlook towards people should be free from any prejudice. He must be equipped with a progressive and development oriented attitude towards the challenges of the day like women empowerment, poverty, illiteracy, malnutrition, human trafficking or racism. Blend with a scientific temper, "modernity" must attempt to find sustainable solutions to the issues rather than creating an issue in its clash with the traditions. Exercising a fine balance of judgment, "modernity" must use the wisdom and direction of the traditions and customize it to present times to deliver justice for the under privileged sections of the society.

Traditions form an inextricable part of our social fabric. They seep into an individual during his upbringing inadvertently. There are traditions which are specific to family or caste or even to the entire society. While some traditions die down silent death in face of changing times and their rigidity, others blossom and spread over larger domains. Instead of being skeptical, hesitant or ashamed in following norms of tradition, the trend to flaunt and promote the traditional values and customs is beckoning the present generation. Traditional folk music and classical dances are finding popular acceptance at the modern world stage, while traditional dishes of different regions are vetting appetites of communities globally. Ceremonies, like karvachauth, which were limited in their spread, have now been accepted across communities as the mobile present day population interacts with a larger segment of society.

Print, electronic, social and e-media have also contributed to viral spread of traditional customs and values. Bhangra and Dandiya are no more confined to a particular region. Similarly, modernity can never come in the way of us forsaking the celebration of our festivals. Festivals are the celebration of our traditional values and customs. The scale of display and extravagance related to most festivals might change in sync with times but the core ethos of tradition imparts them with the real glow. Modernity has lent festivals a commercial touch but the joy and togetherness associated with them is a blessing of traditions. Families may spend excessively on decorations and fireworks, in differing capacities, on a Diwali night, but the common thread of family puja joins them all to the richness of inherited traditions. Without the traditional family rituals, every festival would appear hollow. Modernity has lent a different flavor to the manner of celebration of these festivals but tradition keeps their soul alive. They will continue to symbolize the beautiful blend of these concepts.

The clashes with the modern pattern of approach to the issues have often turned violent and ugly. Traditional wisdom must be a guiding light for the generations and not become suffocating for the individual's existence at any time. The free spirit of humanity must be respected and individual's choice to chart his own destiny, even to violation of tradition, must be upheld. In the tradition of following a particular family business, an individual's passion for some other profession should not be stifled. His "modernity" in this case is his talent or belief in charting his own destiny which must be given a chance. In case of failure, tradition must welcome back to the folds with open arms and heart. The "youth" like exuberance of "modernity" has to be tempered by sagacity and serenity of "grand father" like tradition.

Traditional thoughts or manner of approach to the problems of society will have to be tweaked to suit the present world realities. It must not be taken as blasphemous, rather as a necessity of evolution. Modernity is all about being in step with the changing times - constantly evolving and adapting. Traditional authoritarian styles of leadership have evolved to modern participative approach in domain of management styles. Traditional roles of women in most societies have changed as they begin to take bigger responsibilities and contribute financially for the family. Issues like the same gotra marriages invoking diktats from khap panchayats or the dressing sensibilities of women should not be commanded over individuals in these changing times. Rather, through debates and discussions between generations, a mature consensual social understanding must be sought on these issues.

The structure of relationships has also undergone changes. Countries have legalized same sex marriages and societies are becoming more expressive about intricacies of relationships. Civil societies are becoming more vibrant globally as greater number of people joins the bandwagon of adult citizenry. All these changes are ensuring that the clashes with the traditional structural order and thought pattern are bound to occur. It is the mature manner in which the people and the politicians deal with such clashes that determines the levels of friendship or animosity between tradition and modernity.

This phase of societal transition, whereby the pace of change has amplified, demands heightened levels of caution. Scholars, intellectuals and academicians will have to proactively debate on various burning issues where traditional thinking is at loggerheads with the modern sensibilities. School and universities will have to emphasize on the relevance of respect for tradition along with creating progressive modern individuals. The policy framers and implementers have the biggest challenge on their hands. They have to uphold the traditional wisdom of ages and mould it into a binding factor rather than them becoming a divisive issue. More intellectual churning in society before framing of policies and a transparent democratic implementation of sensitive issues will become a grave challenge. Instances of moral policing by self appointed messiahs of righteousness have to be dealt with an iron hand. Also the strength of tradition in imparting spiritual growth and instilling discipline must be acknowledged and highlighted from diverse platforms.

The need to develop friendship between tradition and modernity is paramount. It will be in interest of individuals, society and the entire nation. As friends, the present generation would be able to carry forward the baton of traditional thought and wisdom to the coming generations. It is a part of inherited responsibility which each of us must undertake with reverence. Also, the present constraints of reality have to be taken into account by smart incorporation of modern variations.

Various traditional arts and crafts of our nation provide suitable example highlighting prosperity achievable by this collaboration. They have to be protected from dying a silent death and need the onslaught of neglect in this age of modernity. Craft works like silk work of Kanchipuram, patacharita paintings of Odisha, kagzi pottery of Alwar, Jamdani saris of Bengal , bandhini work of Gujarat and numerous others in different parts of the nation are rich embodiments of traditional heritage needing space and platform to prosper. The traditional skill and mannerism of their development is valued globally but only modern means of marketing and financial support can ensure their survival against the reality of globalization. The traditional silk saris of Varanasi will continue to hold relevance but their market acceptability can be enriched manifold if they incorporate the designs prevalent in contemporary market. Though modernity appears at odds with tradition, it also becomes the vehicle to keep the traditional arts and crafts in commercial demand.

The foundation of traditions lends the much vaunted stability to the edifice, but the design built must be in sync with the present day living requirements. In every domain, whether sports, politics, religion, business or conduct of life, the blend would create a dynamic attitude capable of weathering the strongest of the tempest. As friends who are open to suggestions and correct each other's mistakes, good points from traditional wisdom can be grasped and inculcated. This will also prevent the repetition of the past blunders and sieve out the possibilities of failure in any venture. With the contours of tradition acting as guidelines, sufficient space for innovation by modernity must be ensured by governance and society for a peaceful, healthy and inclusive development to materialize.

# Developing a **Sporting Culture** in India

Over the past few decades, with active involvement in major global decisions and events, India has left significant footprint in every arena. On the threshold of achieving the mantle of global leadership, Indian success story is scripted in diverse fields of political debates, economy, social ventures, entrepreneurship, art and culture. However, the domain of sports continues to experience drought of significant Indian presence. The nation of over 1.2bn continues to grapple with ideas to build a sporting culture.

Sports in Indian society have always been viewed as a leisure activity, which is given the "leftover" time, after tending to "more significant" activities. From time immemorial, kings and princes indulged in sports like hunting or chariot racing for the purpose of amusement. Though the global notions about sports underwent a change, the Indian mindset has refused to bring out and expand the place of sports in our society.

Over the past decades, with every passing global sporting event like the Olympics or the Asiads, our attention shifts to the depressing state if Indian sports. This attention span is minimal. As a society, we return to our works for sustenance and in training the upcoming generation to earn their daily bread. For the nation, we expect medals in global events but shirk away from preparing our child to be that medal winner.

The presence or absence of sporting culture in any society is a reflection of several other factors operating simultaneously in the social milieu. India, with huge population as a resource is gifted with a large pool of human resource to draw out talent for different sports. Towns and villages abound with youngsters, whose natural inclination towards sports, can be molded into global sporting personalities. Dhanraj Pillai, Deepika Kumari, Vijender Singh, Sushil Kumar all represent the twinkle eyed youngster from small towns with big aspirations to shine with their talent, when presented with any opportunity. But the names are few enough to be counted on fingertips. A sporting culture would require proliferation of such opportunities, through government and corporate endeavors, to nooks and corners of the nation.

As a developing nation with huge population and debilitating unemployment, "career development" is a major cause of worry for the youth and their parents. The mindset which is rigidly cast in our society expects students to devote themselves unconditionally to books till they emerge out with decent jobs. Studies are considered the sole path to land up a decent job to earn livelihood and raise a family. This route has attained social sanction and any deviation from this standard finds awkward stares, rebukes and obstructions to overcome. For a sporting culture to develop, sports must be viewed as a viable career option in the Indian society.

Parents fail to recognize sports as career option in India. They understood the limited nature of opportunities for the sportsmen at the recognized national level. Only a handful, from amongst a million aspirants, due to several reasons, get to represent the Indian national side in any sport. The remaining becomes part of the crowd, jostling for space to shine at the pinnacle. Any position below the top goes unrecognized and remains non-lucrative to be perused as a career option in sport. But as a society don't we fail to recognize the same situation in other disciplines as well. We are ready to push our children to become mediocre or sub-standard engineers, doctors, lawyers, CAs but not as a sportsman. This reflects upon the challenge in building India into a sporting nation.

Sporting culture will begin to take shape only when an assured career progression system can be charted out for every sport. This will induce confidence in parents to permit their child to follow his sporting passion as a decent earning assurance at every step even below the nationals could be visualized.

Another impediment in the way of building sporting culture is the lack of quality and affordable coaching available for youngsters to pursue their dreams. Most schools fail to provide for a specialized coach for every sport as that will add to the school fees. As sport is not considered as an integrated part of education, this expenditure is viewed as an avoidable burden by the school authorities. They end up hiring a generalist trainer who fails to spot talent for a particular sport and groom the child accordingly. Also, the infrastructure in most schools is found wanting to promote most of the sports. The private coaching centres have recently found space in certain cities. However, the high cost charged by them deters the talented youth from lower and middle class from joining these centres.

The performances in sports at school and college level fail to attract appreciation and recognition. The student is judged only by his ability to obtain marks in academics, which adds to the peer pressure of an aspiring sportsman. He is expected to perform in academics for the social acceptance and additionally find time and energy to shine in the sports coaching academies, simply to justify his interest and ability. This dual expectation burden has nipped several budding sporting talents at the very onset of their careers.

Lack of transparency at various selection levels has also been afflicting the Indian sports. Sincere hard working youth often fail to make the cut in the trials where several unethical practices seem to dominate. Lack of fairness at trials is a big setback to the honest efforts of any sportsman. Feeling of dejection is compounded by the future related uncertainties and social mockery of his abilities.

Absence of a healthy and dependable social security system adds to the resistance in pursuing sports as a career. Any major injury or lack of selector's favourable nod can prolong the period of struggle, characterized by uncertain and meager income source. The healthy social security system of networked schools and health care abroad recognize and support players of the zonal and club levels to the fullest. This state provided assurance promotes a confidence in the society to create space for a sporting culture to proliferate.

The role of administrative bodies also comes under scanner when deliberating upon development of sporting culture. Most of these bodies have become granaries of inefficiency and malfunctioning. Often run as fiefdoms, they prevent the transparent and accountable face of sports to emerge in Indian society. Active role of these administrative bodies with a wider involvement of senior players in decision making can give impetus to sporting culture in India. The proposal to get these bodies under the scanner of RTI is a progressive step to drive away the darkness of inefficiency and unaccountability enveloping these bodies.

With every passing Olympics, we blankly stare at spirit and stamina of global athletes competing for laurel. While US, China and European nations race ahead with medals, our levels of disappointment increase with each passing day. We feel elated even to come on board the medals tally by some spirited efforts. This picture demands a makeover. A makeover which should catapult India onto the sporting map of the world and this demands a collective effort by several stakeholders. The packed stadium euphoria of cricket needs to be replicated in other sports by a determined focus and planned approach.

For any culture to germinate and flourish, the seeds have to be healthy and rich. The recent performances at the Asiads, the Common Wealth Games and other global events portends that the embryo needs to be molded with an eye at the future. China managed to bring about such a flourishing sporting culture in about two decades. The opportune moment in Indian sporting history is now and needs to be grasped with both hands to develop the culture over the next few decades.

Schools are the nurseries of spotting and grooming sporting talent to bring about a makeover to Indian outlook for sports. Marks for sports performances can be an innovative step to create space for more sporting activities. Diversification of sporting activities, by providing sports other than cricket a chance must be taken up in right earnest. Higher frequency of inter and intra school sports meet will generate a competitive spirit amongst the students to shine for their units. Preparation for these meets will ensure focused time and energy spent to bring out the best of the student in the sport of his liking.

The culture of pushing all school kids to play cricket or football in their sports period must change. A focused and scientific approach to identify the sport specific talents and their grooming over a period of time will pay rich dividends over time. Free passes for students to attend sporting events in their cities will have a strong effect in imbibing sporting spirit by students. Schools can arrange interactions of students with performing sports icons of the city to motivate and inspire youth to take to sports.

Every segment of the society must collectively take the responsibility of building the sporting culture. State must ensure that sporting facilities reach to the grassroots through schools and colleges in rural areas. Games like volleyball and handball which require minimal infrastructural support can be taken up on priority basis. Regular recruitment of coaches for schools and colleges must be emphasized and ensured. It is imminent to spread the opportunities to every part of the nation to tap the talent.

Corporate houses can contribute strongly to this cause by sponsoring of mega events. They can aid in causing awareness by publicizing events. Training academies set by MRF and Tata have been doing a yeoman service to the nation by grooming talented and providing them a platform to knock on doors of national selectors. Many products of these academies have shone brightly for the nation at different stages. Certain costly sports need active subsidized coaching either by state or the corporate. Tennis, squash, badminton or shooting have been inaccessible to common masses due to lack of adequate and affordable centre to learn the game. This arena demands active focus by government and corporate. The state government can establish hunt teams to collaborate with district administration to hunt for hidden talent in obscure areas. Swimming talent from ponds of villages and archery from tribes of forest must be tapped by this team through coordination between school authorities, coaches and district administration. Such selected youth must be groomed in sports academies, with lodging and food to develop an Olympian for the nation.

Media and sporting icons have a critical role in building a sporting culture in India. The omnipresent media must highlight the apathy of sports bodies and raise awareness about the need for more systematized career progression in sports. It must play an active role through debates and discussions to attack the mindsets of people and sell sports as a career option.

Cricket caught the imagination of the nation by the active role of 1983 World Cup winning team and the continued stature given to cricketers by media. Cricket should not be viewed as an adversary of the sports in India. Rather lessons can be taken for the popularity of cricket to transform the cricketing culture into sporting culture. There is enough space for other sports to grow and flourish in India along with cricket.

Public memory has a very short span, especially with sports in India because as a nation we are not overly involved with sports. In such scenario, media plays a force multiplier by repeatedly flashing past performances, by interviewing famous cricketers or by holding cricket related debates and discussions. This keeps the cricketers fresh in every one's memory along with the overdose of cricket matches and their "live" coverage. Such planned marketing is supported by frequent successes in cricket which has generated role models like Kapil Dev and Sachin Tendulkar.

With this backdrop and the recent successes of Saina Nehwal, Sushil Kumar, Gagan Narang, Mary Kom media must build up campaign to disseminate a sporting culture. More companies should approach these stars for advertisement campaigns so that their "presence" can be felt by society, promoting any upcoming event through adcampaigns and hoardings and by infusing money in these sports by corporate backing can bring a different scenario altogether. The ripple effect of Vijender Singh's success transformed Bhiwani into a boxing hub. We need more such hubs for athletics, swimming, basketball, hockey and football to emerge in the nation. Saina and Gopichand's success turned attention towards badminton while Leander and Mahesh are looked up to in lawn tennis. The success story of these icons demands continued coverage by media along with their upcoming events, to create space for these sports. These performances must be tracked and details brought to public to allow them to have a look and encourage their child to follow these footprints.

Sports in India need a renewed focus. It is time it moves away from the last pages of newspaper, last period of schools, and last priority of parents for their child's careers and domains of last benchers of schools and colleges. It is time that sporting authorities get a revamp by inclusion of more experienced players in decision making so that they understand requirement of players threadbare. It is time we understand that thrill and pride on hearing the national anthem played when Abhinav Bindra won the gold for India requires sustained efforts, hard work and support from parents. His case was of individuals fight despite the resistance of the system. Imagine how many more Bindras India can produce if the system is supportive, procedures conducive and mindset favourable for a sporting culture to flourish.

# Globalization of **Terror**

The images of collapsing trade towards are etched crystal clear in our memories. Explosions in Madrid and London were heard the world over - repeatedly in the comforts of living rooms. Closer home, serial blasts in Mumbai Malegaon or recent atrocities in Hyderabad were all carried, presented and vividly dissected in scrutiny for our consumption.

Connectivity, we defend, is an asset - a necessity in the modern era. The world is shrinking and the global hub has gifted numerous opportunities and advantages to en cash. But in this rush to capitalize on the fruits of globalization, have we missed its impact on a hostile framework? The role of globalization, both as a cause and vehicle of perpetration of violence is increasingly being realized.

Globalization has revolutionized each and every aspect of our society, touching us at myriad levels in numerous ways. From the times, we decided to jumps on and integrate with global forces by adopting the new economic policy, the pace of changes has only taken a unidirectional approach.

Easing of restrictions on trade barriers and tariffs, introduced an era of competition and quality in the Indian markets. Consumerism has become the order of the day. Nations began to pour in their strengths to capture markets elsewhere. However, the growth story missed the vision from another segment. This market led approach bled the farmers, the weaker and the marginalized sections of our society. Though the fruits of growth percolated to these sections, inequity grew at a rapid pace, creating pockets of grudges, neglect and marginalization.

Globalization brought along an era of instant entertainment through satellite television, ignorant of the sensitivity of the population. Though the barriers of culture and religion were being broken down to build a world of understanding, the process accentuated alienation of certain segments of the society, by sheer irreverence and insensitivity to local traditions, values and cultural uniqueness. The promotion of individuality got replaced by an invasion on ethics and homogenization of the perceived good.

The apathy of the state in an era of market led growth bred indignation in certain segments of society. In face of sheer neglect and socio-economic deprivation, terror emerged in different forms and under different names. Violence was a consequence and globalization provided a vehicle to collaborate their efforts and be heard.

The face of terror remains elusive. We have unfortunately linked it to Islamic terrorism, but that is just one of the several nefarious manifestations, albeit the most global and visible form. Terrorism traces its roots in neglect by the state social, economical or political. Whether ULFA or Maoists or the rebels in Chechenya, they highlight the failure to integrate the section deprived of fruits of globalization into a social and economic security net.

To make their demands heard, violence appeared as an easy alternative to these perverted groups. Internet came to the rescue to fulfill any information starvation. The very medium which revolutionized corporate profits, government efficiency, knowledge banks for researches served the bad master with easy information on arms, ammunitions and bomb-making. Even security details and planning information was utilized by the attackers on parliament from this medium.

Softening of borders in the era of global mobility provided an easy access to recruits. Training camps began operation on a multi-national basis and funding mobilized through a worldwide network. Elements of a global market led economy were visible in the corporate like functioning undertaken by these groups. Camps in Pakistan and Afghanistan thrive on basis of funding from business tycoons of S Arabia. Underworld rackets in India operate with global linkages in Dubai and Malaysia.

Another tool of the global village, grossly misused, is the network of communication. Distances have ceased to be a barrier. Planning, organizing and detailing has attained cross-national dimensions. Recruitment in the name of religious extremist ideology has also become a global phenomenon.

While the liberal visa and travel norms, aimed to facilitate trade, bilateral exchanges and cultural cohesiveness, they have also facilitated recruitment and execution of terror plots. Pakistani suspects in London bombing and Indian youth in Glasgow attacks indicate the massiveness of the cancerous spread. Cutting across boundaries of nations, the tentacles of hatred have spread deep and wide.

Globalization of education has opened a new vista for the student community to learn from the globally recognized centres and prosper by utmost development of their potential. However, the nefarious and destructive mindset can sketch his designs through this opportunity also. Education abroad is aiding wider collaboration, networking and perpetration of extremist ideologies.

No religion promotes violence. It is the misinterpretation for parochial gains by an obsessive mindset which spreads hatred in name of 'holy war'. The perceived injustices are glorified and violence sanctified as religious duty by hardliner clerics. Fragmentation of society, distrust and spread of fear is the purpose and the shrinking globe offers the medium.

Media glorifies acts of violence and the repeated playing of such ghastly acts in name of "active reporting" provides a platform to bring terror straight to our living rooms. Footages of hostage abduction and warnings by terror groups find media as a source of dissemination.

Another aspect of a closer world finds reflection in institutions of security (like NATO, SCO, APEC) or finance (IMF, World Bank). Highlighting integration, dependence and cohesiveness of links, they provide opportunities to such groups to decide and pounce on the vulnerable and affect the entire para-statal. The recent kidnapping of S Korean hostages by a resurgent Taliban to press for their demands is a burning alarm.

Terror has attained vicious dimensions. It is global, elusive and unidentifiable. The enemy is amorphous and could be breeding in any section of the society with globalization; it is empowered and armed to carry out its nefarious motives. While the state is perplexed at the enormity of the problem, the solution may again germinate in a global partnership.

The US led war against terror might have been a reactionary response but it provides a cue to upgrade our approach to mission mode levels and collaborate globally. However, the execution needs a different direction, a novel approach. Flaunting of "might of force" is not a solution to win an ideological war. The enemy in any terror camp across the globe is a hardliner who operates on ground of perceived injustices and deviated psychology. The war could only be won at that level.

'Think Global, Act Local' is often the phrase linked with sustainable efforts and that should form the premise of our efforts. No knee jerk responses ever eliminate the cause. Globalization is a reality. Though it may accept accusations of supporting the evil designs, it cannot be overlooked in modern era. It should rather provide platform to collaborate the national efforts through regional forums like SAARC, G-8, UN, MERCOSUR. Innovative mechanisms, like the 'Joint Terror Mechanism' advocated by our Prime Minister, Dr. Man Mohan Singh, on sidelines of NAM, needs support and effective implementation.

Also, while acting locally, each state should encourage political dialogue with the representatives of these groups to understand the perceived injustice and negotiate the demands. The arms surrender and political integration of Maoists in Nepal could lead the way. Better monitoring mechanisms of the tools of globalization can prevent their use by wrong hands. WTO negotiations regarding tariffs and market access should be sensitive to the needs of those whose livelihood itself is jeopardized in exchange of a higher profit for the other.

A responsible global media and a civil society that is aware and responsive could prevent alienation of any segment of society. Constraints should be strengthened by State, even on pervasive forces of globalization, the moment they encroach the liberty of any individual. Internet should be used by educational institutions to spread awareness about teachings of our holy books and drive home the message that no religion supports violence in any forms. Stricter vigilance and information sharing within the nation and across nations can thwart many designs of destruction.

Globalization, moderated by consideration for people, should institutionalize peace and harmony. It can work as a unifying force to uproot the evil intentions. Global funds to develop the deprived regions and stricter monitoring of any human right violations anywhere in the world could prevent growth of any cluster of neglect. Global forces should bolster efforts of state to militate against apathy, neglect, hunger, illiteracy and ignorance. Ethic and religious differences should be given a lifeline of negotiation and accommodation.

The responsibilities, both of an individual and a nation, have grown in face of diminishing isolated and growing terror. Economic aspect notwithstanding, the call of the hour is moral awakening and resurgence of humanity. The strength of our culture and heritage faces the test of globalization, whereby it should emerge as an anchor for global development. Let our efforts find directions to develop a global village - a sustainable model of peace, tolerance and harmony.

# Corruption in **India**

A beautiful wooden house by the side of the lake added to the completeness of the exquisite landscape. The strong structure had withstood the vagaries of nature in form of torrential rainfall, terrible thunderstorms and devastating hail and snowfall. Lavish praises were endowed on the structural strength and foundational firmness of the house. To utter surprise and dismay of many, the house collapsed in the stillness of spring. Termites had eaten through the structure rendering it hollow and vulnerable. In our nation beset with multitude of challenges and problems, the cancerous spread of corruption holds a similar threat.

The much debated phenomenon of corruption has permeated every plausible sphere of our dealings in society. It is not a recent origin phenomenon, but has certainly assumed monstrous proportions, sufficient to destabilize any society. It has existed globally ever since humans decided to settle down in a social set up. Norms and rules were decided and adopted by a social consensus, which invariably gave rise to a breed of deviants. The moral debates of right versus wrong soon gave the platform to demystify the deviations. As the righteous path became arduous, taxing and challenging, the breed of fickle-hearted expanded choosing the easier path which satisfied their material needs, albeit by nailing their morals.

The institutionalized nature assumed by corruption has the potential to choke the life of the nation. It becomes more dreadful as the social stigma attached to theses deviations has been losing ground. It is glorified in informal circles and in a surprising state of "mass- surrender" has been often branded as a "way of life" in the contemporary Indian society. As a civilization which prides itself in values and culture, have we collectively blown out the candles of hope to redeem our society from this ailment?

At every level of interaction of common man with the system- schools and colleges admission, applications for basic amenities, policing, licensing authorities, promotion, tax departments - corruption is breeding like a norm, rather than an aberration. At the heart of every such corrupt system, lie the individuals who are morally bereft and lack ant commitment to the values of their job profiles. They expect to gain their illegal extraction from the hard earned income of other only by virtue of their occupancy of a post and other person's imminent need to get his work done. It is an exploitation of the worst order. Sadly, we have stopped even recognizing it!

Does justifying the cancerous spread of corruption as "need" of struggling individuals hold any gravity? Or have we, as a society, managed to blur the defining lines between need and greed? Corruption by public sector employees often finds vocal defense by citing their insufficient pay. With inflation making essential commodities out of reach of a common man, he looks for avenues to augment his income to raise his family.

In a largely patriarchal social setup, where most women stay home and fail to contribute to financial security of the household, the buck rests with the male-earning member only. Added to this gender disparity is the twin problem of lack of entrepreneur culture and unemployment, which further strains the earning member of the family to feed larger mouths only through his efforts.

The weak social security set up adds to the forces that often drive a strong willed honest employee to sacrifice his morals. With a number of expectations from the family regarding children education, saving for their marriages and gifts, health related emergencies and desire to have a permanent abode before retirement, the regular income is seen highly insufficient. With rising gap between salaries and inflated market prices of the products, a monthly salary leaves no scope for futuristic security of any kind. This is where a stable social security system guaranteeing along with pension, some assured benefits of education, health and housing can drive away fears of future, which will influence the behavior of present.

Public sector employees also justify their corrupt acts by lamenting about the obscene gap in pays being received by them and their counterparts in the private sector. Although some regulation can be sought for maintaining value for money, the public sector employee must appreciate the several incentives, beyond pay, which he utilizes as the part of the system. An appreciation of the harmony between the public and private sector must also seep in by appreciation of their diverse work in a common effort of nation building. Rather than profit garnering, it is the spirit of public service which has been supreme in these organizations and a similar sentiment must be appreciated, cherished and reflected by each employee.

However, even to deliver the rights of the citizen and to perform the basic duties of their post, at a pace expected of them, they expect something extra to whet their appetite.

The comparisons with the private sector and with their own colleagues indulging in this nefarious habit results in sustained trauma and mental fatigue for the employee. The pressures from family and social sanction to this "low risk: high gain" indulgence tests the commitment to values and integrity of the person. These are the testing times of dilemma, where many individuals prove weak and surrender before the temptations. The desire to raise their standard of living and arrange for future themselves due to weak social security structures by state perpetuates the phenomenon of corruption further deep.

Corruption is no more a sector-specific phenomenon. It is equally rampant in the private sector where it is "managed" in a systematized and proficient manner. However, the impact of corrupt practices of government employees is far consequential. A recent survey highlighted that the nation is compromising on about 1.5% of GDP growth due to the widespread existence of corruption. A nation with more malnourished children than the poorest regions of sub-Saharan Africa and which still has highest number of illiterates just can not afford to go this way. This debilitating effect on growth hits hard on our development strategy whereby we expect the growth to trickle down and deliver fruits at the bottom of the pyramid.

It is corruption related leakages which made an Ex-Prime Minister remark that of a rupee spent by the central government, only ten paise manages to reach the targeted beneficiary of the scheme. But over the years, have we cared to trace out and plug the leakages of the remaining substantial chunk of the pie? Policies of any government are the tools which help in delivering value to the society. Inspite of perfectly framed policies, our progress in improving our social indicators of health, education and sanitation have been tardy. The leakages of corruption have driven holes in the fabric of effective governance. The policies manage to perform only on paper but loose their sheen when applied on the ground level.

In this way, it is the poor who is hit the hardest by the menace of corruption in the state implementation machinery. We need not be surprised if this sustained exploitation and neglect of the weak evaporates his faith from the government machinery and democratic institutions. Corruption lies at the heart of problems where the oppressed citizens have taken to arms against the state.

Corruption has not only been making the government schemes ineffective, it has been also playing with he lives of innocents. Adulteration of essential food items and drugs has claimed multiple lives. Health care infrastructure remains inadequate in rural India, despite allocations due to pilferages in the amount. Corruption in awarding of tenders has resulted in collapsing bridges, dilapidated roads and projects yielding cost and time over-runs. Corruption in every stage of any large industrial project setup deters the investors and leaves disastrous impact on industrialization and trade.

Transparency International, a global civil society organization, leading the fight against corruption has ranked India at 94 out of 176 countries in Corruption Perception Index. With such global perception, we are paying high price for this moral weakness of individuals. Corruption is incapacitating the much valued human resource of India by blocking the flow of sufficient food and nutrition to them. The saga of food delivery through PDS is a rotten tale of corrupt individuals exploiting the system to their benefits. Simultaneously, the material resources have also fallen into the kitty of the corrupt lobby of rich and powerful. The resources mean to deliver dividends to all citizens of nation are being siphoned off to the benefit of a few.

Corruption in contemporary India has attained obscene magnitudes. The exposure of a number of scams in recent years has re-established the unholy nexus of business - politician - bureaucrat in exploiting their positions for personal gains. Political corruption has touched unimaginable extremes with an almost unapologetic misuse of hard earned tax-payers money. The illegally earned money is filling coffers in foreign accounts of the rich and the powerful. Can we still fathom to argue the "need" basis of these massive thefts from the common man's money? Do we apply the same standards to defend corruption done by a constable struggling to raise his family and a minister overloading his Swiss bank account/ it simply boils down to lack of integrity, lack of respect for the responsibility associated with one's job and weak moral grounding of the individual.

Tackling of corruption demands an entire generation of strong willed and determined individuals supported by few effective legislations and a vibrant civil society determined to root out this evil. Resignation to corruption as a way of life has to be a thing of the past. It is the people who have been greasing the palms of the corrupt and its their power which has the potential to reform the system. They have been yielding as it is tough for a common man to comprehend and tackle the system by devoting his time and energy in pursuing the honest applications which are unaccompanied by the greenbacks.

The maze of bureaucratic procedures befuddles a common man, who yields to pay more to keep his file hopping from one table to another. Simplification of these procedures and transparency about them, along with fixing accountability is the first step towards uprooting corruption. India has already made a beginning through RTI, which needs to be strengthened over time by relentless public pressure on the governments of the day.

People have found it easier to give as they lost faith on the efficacy of system to operate on its own without greasing palms at each level.

## "Power corrupts; absolute power corrupts absolutely"

This eroded confidence has to be restored by preventing concentration of power in few hands. With proper computerized file tracking systems in place, accountability of individuals can be ascertained with accuracy. The social approval to this practice should be diminished by simple measures like announcing names of the most corrupt official on monthly basis, based on the feedback from the common public. With the ease of facilitation as criteria, the public can also indicate the nature of their interaction with any employee of the department and thereby bring openness in the system.

Technology can prove to be an able warrior in this crusade against corruption. The success of computerization has already been felt in several departments like passport booking and railway reservation and can be extended to others with ease. Basic training of manpower in operating systems can unfold an era of opportunities even for the most remotely located individuals and save them from corrupt clutches of middlemen. Computerization will help in doing away with unrequired human intervention which becomes a node of corruption in the chain of service delivery. Similarly, single window clearances for projects will also go a long way in restoring confidence of investors and provide him a hassle free environment of operation.

The "low risk" element associated with corruption must be targeted in particular to create a deterrence value in performing any such act. Any highlighted act of corruption must entail strict and immediate punishment. With more special fast track courses, these cases must be disposed off on a priority basis. Increased conviction rate can bring about deterrence effect in the society. Raids by a proactive IT department targeting any disproportionate assets will also have similar effect.

Political corruption needs to be wiped out by opening a war on several fronts. Electoral reforms are the imminent call of the nation and only adequate reforms will ensure that right spirited people manage to reach the positions of power. Only the candidates with a transparent and clean track record and experience in social work should be promoted by adequate awareness about candidate.

Democratization of political parties is another fundamental requirement to prevent involvement of money in cornering a party ticket. More transparency in party procedures can be desired by the election commission. A system of regular audit and tracking of party funds also need to be established. Funding of election expenses have also promoted the clandestine collaboration of business houses with political parties which later seek favor from the party when in power. State funding of elections can be viable alternative which can be worked over.

In a mission mode approach, the need of hour is to bring strong legislations and then working on them to transform the grassroots spread of corruption. To detoxify the entire body, the crusaders need support through an armed Whistleblower Protection Bill. Efforts to expose and bring back the nations wealth stashed abroad must be intensified. With a potent Judicial Standards & Accountability Bill, corruption in judiciary must be stemmed, so that it remains the cornerstone of every citizen's faith and trust. Irregularities in awarding og government contracts can be given a death blow by bringing in the public procurement law. All efforts should be guided towards reducing discretion of public authorities and establishing transparent procedures.

The biggest strength that this anti-corruption movement can derive is by challenging the mindsets of the individuals. It is an arduous task and may consume an entire generation but it is the most sustainable way of eradicating corruption from India's future.

"Charity begins at home". At home, only the child picks up his first lessons which become an intrinsic part of him as he grows up into an individual. The small moral deviations that parents initiate a child into unknowingly, branch into a rigid flowering tree later, whereby the individual fails to acknowledge and see any wrong in his deviations from the rightful path. The rich Indian value system is the ultimate weapon to counter the menace of corruption. The values of integrity, ethics and honesty should be part of natural training of any young mind.

The onus lies on every school and college teacher, training academies for bureaucrats and every parent to implant it in joining minds that the path of righteousness, however difficult it might seem, is the one God desires his children to take. With such moral grounding, the child will grow up into a strong individual who will happily undergo hardship but refuse to sell his morals at the drop of hat. Corruption is "the" biggest problem afflicting our motherland and roots of several other problems can be traced back to it. Other problems then merely appear as symptoms of this deviation from the righteous path. Contain this to eliminate it. Do not accept this as a way of life.

The recent Lokpal debate, which took the nation by storm, requires careful deliberation. The existing institutional framework must be fine tuned and strengthened at all the levels of operation. Role of CAG and Anti Corruption Cells in different departments must be strengthened. Sufficient operational autonomy to CVC and CBI will go a long way in striking at the root of the problem. A vibrant and demanding civil society can instill political will, which has been slow to emerge on its own. The Anna Hazare led movement should be a platform for a sustained demand to establish an effective institution of Lokpal and LokAyuktas.

However, establishment will only be a necessary but not sufficient step. Civil society organizations must create an atmosphere of awareness amongst citizens about their rights and provide forums to register any complaints of corruption. Each such complaint should be looked into, made public and the corruption demanding culprit be convicted through proper channels. This demands a brigade of committed anti-corruption warriors from amongst the society. Much onus lies on the youth as they create an India for their tomorrow. An India with enormous opportunities and a nation, which devoid of corruption, holds potential to scale the unscaleable glory.

# Ideology or Technology

A tiny seed holds the potential to feed an entire family. As the essence and richness of a seed finds suitable conditions to germinate, it blossoms into a storehouse of magnanimity. Changes in the society breed in ideas. These ideas find translation into action in a suitable governance environment. It is this translation which eventually proves the worth of an idea. In cases of ideas enjoying a popular support, technology acts as a catalyst to enhance the effectiveness of application of the ideology for larger good of the society.

Ideas have power to bring revolutions and topple dynasties. Histories of nations stand testimony to the strength that an innocuous idea can gather and the course of destiny it charts for the society. As idea gains popular currency, it can brew an uprising or rewrite social contract for the land. They blossom into ideologies, supported by intellectuals and utilized in the minefield of politics by astute leaders. The conviction of a nation in a particular ideology begins to underline the trajectory of its story.

Ideology, just like technology, is the product of mental churning. Science resides in every action and particle of this universe. However, the knack to transform the dreary scientific principles and equations into tool of technology is the product of an ingenious human mind. While ideologies spurned from the mental hullaballoo have more value connotations, technology as a facilitator devises ways for effective and unbiased distribution of that value in the society. It is the synergy of their constructive mix which has the potential to positively alter the way of life for individuals.

Different schools of thought, backed by intellectuals, are supporter of different ideologies for conduct of governance of the state. The norms of social contract in the society develop accordingly. These norms define parameters for conduct of interactions, means of production, economic guidelines and rules of engaging with the government. In any stable society, the order is dictated by the accepted ideology of state which must result in a minimal incremental enhancement in quality of life of the citizens. The absence of such enrichment becomes the cause of discontent.

The seeds of change germinate on grounds of discontentment. The "status quo" of the prevailing order and its underlying ideology faces the questions by a rising tide of dissent. Another rung of intellectuals promote an alternative ideology in this period of societal upheavals. Old orders are broken down. New rules of the game are framed. Structural changes are carried out to facilitate the processes in this new ideological backdrop. Often the heads of tyrants also roll down in such ideological landscape transformation. However, the intention behind all such churnings deserves attention. Ideology fails to strike chord unless it delivers a hope of a better quality of life for the individual. This hope is the essence of acceptance or rejection of any ideology.

Quality of life of citizens is the litmus test about the effectiveness of any ideology. It is this test which demands a fruitful translation of the tenets of any ideology into benefits for larger section of the society. An ideology may be perfect in the domain of grey cells but its' ultimate utility is judged only in harsh domains of ground realities by the quality of its application. It is this aspect of judgment where the tools of technology step in to complement the ideology. The spread achieved by technology aids the depth of ideology for the benefit of society.

Every ideology has space for a specific technology to breed and deliver accordingly. Technology, as a tool ensures optimum utilization of resources of that society, within the ideological contours decided by the state. The technologies for better oil exploration in the Gulf nations or bio-fuel development in Brazil developed to deliver prosperity to the societies without challenging the ideological designs of these states. Transcending the borders of ideology, the technology to locate potential fishing banks is helping the capitalist coast of the USA and the communist coastline of Cuba without any distinction.

The tool of technology is apolitical and unbiased. Over ages, like a loyal servant of the scientific masters, it has simplified numerous procedures and lives. The very strength of this tool is its neutrality. It has never been subservient to any particular ideology and should not be dragged to deepen the ideological fissures. Rather it must mend fissures and divides of class, gender, race and religions.

The prevailing ideology of any state has marked influence on the nature of technology it promotes. Amongst the myriad areas of research, ideology of the state dictates the priority of focus areas. The bitter ideology of one up man ship during the era of Cold War led to major advancements in defense technology for both USA and Soviet Union. Huge budget allocations and acumen of scientists was invested in building up the military might of the nation. Space exploration also spurred a race for supremacy and the power blocs focused on outsmarting the other through better technology. The Cold War to establish the supremacy of either capitalist or communist ideology was executed by innovating smarter technology. The triumph of market led "choice" model over the "communes" was crystallized by fragmentation of Soviet Union. Just like technology, ideology too runs its course.

The entropy in any society is settled when the transition from one ideological contour to another is achieved smoothly. Ideological acceptance and triumph is a contextual concept. It varies from time to time. There is no constancy in its applicability over time and space. Unless the ideology manages to deliver qualitatively to the grassroots, it is bound to crumble in due course. This flexibility to evolution is essential for survival of any ideology. Technology can likewise be tweaked to deliver fruits of development to the citizens of the society.

China's growth over the past few decades highlights a pragmatic approach of synchronized evolution of ideology and technology. To carry a large population base and deliver growth, it maintained focus on rapid development of manufacturing technology. Technology related to automation of plants, advancements in assembly line procedures, workshop and management technologies led to rapid industrialization. This transformed the huge manpower resource into an asset for the nation and also furthered the ideological tenets of the reigning party. Even the mammoth expenditure on modernization of military might and infrastructure by China is in line with an eye on future, where these parameters become critical for claiming global leadership.

The Indian society has traditionally been an agro based primarily rural society. The growth of our nation is inextricably linked to the development of our villages. This ideological focus always emphasized on agricultural and farm based technologies. Despite the small size of land holdings, researches in the field of better agricultural tools like combined harvester and threshers, high yielding variety of seeds, economical irrigation technologies, dry land farming methodologies, coastal land reclamation and promotion of alternative livelihood means for diversification of agriculture have better potential to deliver fruits of development and social justice for larger base of population.

In the backdrop of socialism as leading ideology of that time, industrial development relied heavily on foreign collaborations and investments in large scale Public Sector Units (PSUs) and factories. Heavy machinery for bulk production in plants and factories defined the order of the era as the role of state was considered critical to provide employment opportunities and similar wages. As grains of sand ran down the glass hour, it was realized that PSUs had become white elephants of Indian economy. Later as the ideological contours ushered in policy support for Information Technology and electronics, technology took no time to gain ground in the market. It soon flooded the market with televisions, Video Cassette Recorders, Audio Players and other gadgets according to the diktats of policy which pumped sufficient funds accordingly.

The opening of economy and the market led growth ideology tempered with a commitment to inclusive growth aims to provide greater goods to greater number at the bottom of pyramid. With such pressing constraints of ideology, technological investments always had a humane concern as its' guiding light. Affordability issue of high end technology would introduce class divide in the user segment and cater only to "haves" of the society. This is where the state must step in periodically with options like the low cost Aakash tablets. Such subsidized interventions would help in dissemination of technology to all classes of society and prevent technology from creating a divide in society. This would justify the stated ideological philosophy of "inclusive growth".

Advancement in satellite technology has added to the delivery of vital services to the needy. Resource mapping to decide the best land use, weather forecasting to keep the fishermen off the stormy oceans, soil testing to decide the best choice of fertilizers, telemedicine to deliver healthcare to remotest locations, village resource centers for numerous queries of farmers and tele-education are all highlights of technology delivering social justice in our nation.

There have also been instances of clashes between the ideological framework of state and the performance of prevailing technology. As automation stepped up in factories to improve economy and efficiency of production, huge work force had to be laid off. In nations struggling to provide employment opportunities to a burgeoning youth population, automation in wake of globalization was seen as a curse. However, the bigger picture tells a different story. Instead of castigating technology and blaming it for increasing unemployment, a positive view of the situation puts things in better perspective.

Automation is always the need of time to compete and thrive in a globalized world. It improves economy of production and helps the industry to survive and perform in the competitive scenario. Better production yields better profits and hence higher contribution to growth of the nation. It is the fruits of this growth which percolate to improve lives of these factory workers and also create more employment opportunities for them. Also technological changes come as a challenge for the workforce to upgrade their skills and remain relevant in this progressive world. Thus, such technological changes introduces best use of resources - manpower or capital; create employment in longer run and helps in qualitative growth of both the individual and the society.

The influence of technology on ideology cannot be ignored either. Technology opens up new vistas and has potential to give a new course of direction to the prevailing ideologies. In the march of civilization on the face of this planet, application of science either by accident or design has formed the backbone of progress. The era of nomadic existence of early man transformed to a new ideological framework of settled agriculture after the scientific discovery of fire. Invention of wheels and its' application in locomotion further broadened the evolving dimensions of human thought process. Technology kept opening newer, unknown and unexplored frontiers for humanity providing it with continuous challenge to form suitable social norms accordingly. The ideological contours developed thereby gave further impetus to better utilization of resources through technological advancements. The complementarities of these products of human thought process have led the civilization from one pedestal of development to another.

The world is shrinking. And the global village superimposes an umbrella ideology over the exclusive individual ideologies of nations and societies. A nation can afford to neglect its preparedness for this ideology at its own peril. In the contemporary era, it is the ideology of globalization which has emerged as the major challenge for economies of the world. The internal rules of the game have been altered by each nation accordingly. It was the growing technological advancements which ushered this ideological robe on every nation. Sophistication of IT technologies led to shrinking borders and diminishing barriers. Trade found new platform through portals and e-commerce. Exchange of data and security related challenges assumed global dimensions. As such an era of global hub dawned riding a wave of technological advancements, nations became vary of new opportunities and challenges. Individual ideologies of nations were reframed in context of unleashing of global energies. They had to be synchronized with the over arching ideology of globalization. The competition would value smart utilization of resources and skills with only the fittest surviving at the end of the day. The tables had been turned this time. This challenge has been thrown at the ideological doorsteps by technology. To sail through this successfully smart society will have to reform on aligning the strengths of ideology and technology. The aim of both these tools of change is to facilitate a simpler way of life and a richer quality of life. The tussle, if any, which surfaces is merely cosmetic and ends up in re-invoking a new stable order of peace, justice and development of society.

# Indian **Democracy**

**'Where the mind is without fear and head held high.**
**Into that heaven, my father let my country awake.'**

The vision expressed in the above lines stems from a deep desire to build a fair, just, progressive and inclusive society ; A vision to transform the vast potential of a nation into opportunities for all. It was not a utopian imagination or wild wish, rather a pragmatic assessment of unlimited potential which a newly independent nation can unleash. With a rich and detailed constitution as the guiding light, a democratic India was poised for glory and greatness.

In the small journey as an independent nation, democracy has been the cornerstone of Indian success saga. From the time when doubts were cast on the ability of our survival as a nation to an era when powers across the global look for our guidance, India has travelled miles. The firm foundations of the largest functioning democracy in world have shown myriad results in an effort to create an empowered society.

The representative democracy of India draws strength from a rich constitution, institutions of integrity and a vibrant society. Though it may appear as a simplistic procedure of electing your representative through votes, the ethos it entails on the society is much richer and deeper. It strengthens and empowers 'we the people' and acknowledges the importance of each individual of society.

The smooth transition of governments witnessed by independent India on basis of power of ballots has been a testimony to the real functioning democracy. While our neighbors have struggled with political instability, Indian democracy has risen to become a role model at the global platform. In spite of multitude of problems like illiteracy, poverty, malnourishment and infrastructural deficit India has managed to ensure that political masters remain committed to the right cause.

The entitlement of universal adult franchise has been the base for our democratic success. With reduction of voting age from 21 to 18, Indian democracy was further strengthened as it recognized role of youth in nation building process. Irrespective of a stratified society, people of all caste, colour, creed, language religion, region queue up in a single line to express their choice on the Election Day. This equitous approach has been the strength of Indian democracy.

The functioning of our democracy has ensured that people judge the working of their representatives every five years. With votes, people attach expectations and aspirations. The anti-incumbency rates have many times justified the 'real' power of people. Democracy, as a means, ensures that the political position remains an instrument to serve needs of one and all in society.

Indian democracy has gone from strength to strength. With passing of 73rd and 74th Amendment Acts, democratic decentralization percolated to the grassroots. The Municipalities and Panchayati Raj Institutions have brought governance closer to people. They have empowered the people by giving an elected forum to bring about local level development. Democracy brought new vibrancy through local governance to enable rapid socio-economic progress in the villages.

The rise of coalition polities also marks an indication that regional aspirations of the people are finding a legitimate forum. Political parties have become a medium for expression in an increasingly aware and demanding society. The synergy of several institutions has enabled the democracy to survive multiple onslaughts from different quarters. The judiciary continues to carry impeccable faith and trust of people for protecting their rights. Democratization of judiciary has brought it closer to people through the concept of Public Interest litigation. (PIL)

Democracy is an empowering value. It multiplies the individual's choice and opens plethora of opportunities for every person in society. Democracy believes in rule of law and our judiciary has thwarted every attempt by authoritative individuals or institutions to encroach upon personal rights of citizens. Through various landmark judgments, it has upheld the democratic flavour in the society.

The election commission has functioned as the lifeline of Indian democracy with daunting challenges posed by each successive election. The institution has stood as a bulwark against any nefarious attempt to belittle the voice of people. With effective deployment of security machinery, polling related violence incidents have witnessed a decreasing trend.

The introduction of Election Voting Machines (EVM) is yet another effort to translate wish of people into genuine representation. It eliminates the mass scale bogus voting or invalidity of votes due to improper stamping. Indian democracy manages to exhibit strength of facing and overcoming any challenge to its survival.

The era of liberal markets and a vibrant civil society have increased the liberty of individual. It has brought an era when voice of people can no longer be drowned by the powerful and the oppressive. Media Campaigns and NGOs take up issues of arbitrariness and injustice to any segment of society. The growing strength of media and civil society has been a vital influence to further Indian democracy. Rights of people in obscure villages or tribal belts were often neglected or trampled upon by insensitive apathy. Media campaigns have given voice to people to demand accountability from their representatives.

Right to Information has been a landmark change with potential to revolutionize the entire framework of secretive and inefficient governance. It furthers democratic ethos by arming individuals with right to demand accountability and transparency from the administration. The increasing use of e-governance and Information Technology platforms for delivery of services strengthens democratic access to values. The melting of interface eliminates the discretion of officials, which was a stumbling block in the democratic distribution of values in society.

Though the journey in making democracy a way of life has seen glowing success, several challenges still raise their heads. The distribution of values in the society has been skewed and gaps multiplied post liberalization. It is here that that state needs to step up and play a leading role. State must channelize the resources towards building an inclusive society by creative use of energies of various players.

Media must maintain the standards and values expected from it as a repository of people's hopes and aspirations. With sufficient self regulation to curb paid news and sensationalism, it must emerge as the voice of aam aadmi and enrich Indian democracy. The proactive work of civil society either through social audit of government programmes or highlighting administrative excesses must continue.

A vital component of democratic ethos is the access to the resources for the benefit of community. The State has to uphold the rights of people, especially the marginalized and disempowered, to prevent vaporization of trust. The twist and governance deficit has already generated enough tensions for the nation to handle. Deepening the reach of democracy can be a crucial element of the strategy to handle the menace of Naxalism.

Education has to play a key role in furthering the reach of Indian democracy not only by encouraging the people to participate in the electoral process, but also by asking them to vote for growth and development. The highly stratified Indian society has given birth to casteism as a key distortion in the true reach of democracy. People often end up voting a caste, rather than casting their votes. Even political parties have built upon this divide to create vote-banks. This development militates against the spirit of democracy. While politics gets biased and blindfolded, the holistic development fails to materialize.

Education can raise awareness about the profile of candidate and the development orientation exhibited in his previous stay. Election Commission has to play a proactive role in this arena. It must also ensure that transparency in funding procedure and distribution of tickets becomes sine qua-non for contesting elections. The civil influence of money and criminalization has to be wiped off as a stain from the fabric of Indian democracy.

The executive carries the deep responsibility of maintaining the vitality and richness of Indian democracy. Healthy parliamentary discussion and debates, inclusive policies and programmes and bringing transparency in functioning of administration are the essentials of a demanding society. Legislations like Right to Education also restore the trust of citizens in the functioning of democracy.

The need to bring in the culture of viewing politics as a medium to serve is imminent. The fruits of a growing India must reach all sections of society to maintain trust in this participative process. The planning has to ensure that people remain central in any plan and their voice is recognized in both planning and execution. The democratic decentralization of Panchayati Raj Institutions has to be empowered by autonomy of functions, functionaries and finances bestowed upon them.

Indian democracy has managed to survive challenges from several quarters over the years. With changing time of growing complexities and demands, the attitudinal change of respecting individuality and choice has to be evolved in every quarter. Democracy, as a value, should become the norm of daily functioning of individuals and institutions. Assertive citizens, empowered with information, cannot be denied with this fundamental virtue and any such attempt would only increase impatience and liberalism in the society. The progress of democracy, in spirit and functioning, has been a journey in India. The journey must continue as democracy can only enrich itself progressively. Obstacles, which challenge Indian democracy as a myth will vaporize, as the commitment of Indians is resolute. India democracy will continue to guide the progress of nation to a position of strength in global arena and in delivering an 'inclusive' society.

# Our Future on This Planet

**"There is mercy in every place**
**And mercy, encouraging thought.**
**Gives even affliction a grace**
**And reconciles man to his lot"**

True to the sentiments expressed by the playwright, the gentle showers of earth's mercy has nourished and nurtured the human existence on this planet. Like pampered sons, we have received unidirectional blessings from nature. Unmindful of our intentions, the Mother Earth presented us with plenty to even assuage our griefs and disappointments. But our refusal to grow-up and hold the responsibility baton has tested the clock of nature.

The breach of faith is a huge setback in any relationship. Our unmindful exploitation of the natural resources has tested the generation limits of our planet. The cordial coexistence has assumed the shape of a tussle, as we debate the future of humanity on our planet.

Planet earth provided for the most congenial environment for human existence. The primitive societies, with their limited needs, were content to garner them from the womb of the planet. The societies grew and the problems magnified. Industries stepped-in as temples of growth to satisfy the needs of one and all. The rest, as is said, is history.

The engines of growth rolled on, oblivious of their impacts. Monomaniac man had only profits and growth in his vision. He exploited every facet of the richness of nature-land, water, biodiversity and sources of energy till nature bled and exhausted the supply of mercy. Human Population, itself, has become the biggest question mark on the future of man. The population-resource imbalance is enormously unfavorable for sustenance of humanity. The basic survival needs of food, water, shelter are all in crises due to our growing number.

Food security is a potent threat to the teeming millions. The limits to expansion of agriculture, along with our unsustainable land use, have brought us to the brink of disaster. Sustainability demands that our actions are embroiled in a concern for our future generation. However, indiscriminate use of chemical fertilizers and pesticides and unsuitable cropping practices have exhausted our soil resource. The food productions have stagnated globally. Rapid urbanization and diversion of land for commercial purposes have accentuated the crisis. As the global warming takes over, food production will suffer due to uncertainties of rainfall regime. The human preparedness remains an issue of concern.

The warming itself is our very own creation. The monster which has grown into an intellectual challenge for the global community, took shape under our actions and greed. The overdependence on fossils fuels in an indiscriminate luxury oriented approach enveloped us in a blanket which has become too heavy to bear.

The lungs of our planet - the very symbols of life, our forests, became the victims of the blatant exploitative greed of humanity. These resources were enriching our soils and ameliorating our climate as a faithful friend in the human growth story. But the expansionist drive saw the blades run down rich reserves of food, fuel and fodder.

Vaporization of huge forest reserves sucked the vitality of human existence. The nourishment of soil was threatened and loose soil spread the desolate landscape of deserts on the face of earth. The charging of aquifer stagnated and the ground water level has been receding.

Urbanization brought along its own share of problems. The fault was not in the process but the pace and the unmindful nature which accompanied the menace. While solid waste management of cities remains deplorable, attacking our land resources, water extraction through pumps has been reckless. The growing number of vehicles in the urban jungle has added layers of toxic, choking us and the atmosphere.

Industries contributed to the cause by irresponsible discharge of chemicals in the water bodies killing the flora and fauna of marine ecosystem. The view was always parochial, short sighted and immediate goals were the focus. A vision and holistic approach was missing and the links between actions and their effects took time to dawn. This time gap proved detrimental.

Biodiversity, the very richness of the life on planet, showed signs of crises. While the tankers had spilled enough to stifle marine biodiversity, other habitats were also not pristine. Humanity, in search of resources to build its growth, had exploited every corner. The corals were dying, tigers vanishing but humans failed to trace the link to the things to come.

The human approach to growth and prosperity has always turned a blind-eye to environment and its replenishment. Such consciousness has been considered as a domain of activists and a hurdle to the growth process.

**'There is enough for everyone's need but not for anyone's greed'.**

Mahatma was accurate in his observation and the visionary could predict the direction of human progress. The lesser mortals even failed to follow his advice. Sustainability in the use of resources has been neglected by one and all.

Sustainable development is the crying need of the hour for ensuring the future of humanity on this planet. The understanding has to dawn that we have delayed the efforts already, as global warming knocks on our doors. It is only one of the signals from the nature, that the time to act sensibly is imminent and ticking away.

A glance at our growth story will showcase myriad of pot holes. The process has widened the gulfs in our society and alienated segments from reaping the fruits of development. It has turned a blind eye to deletion of fossil fuels and the heavy accumulation of green house gases. It is time to switch over to sustenance in our activities and in our attitude.

The melting glaciers, erratic rainfall patterns, threats of disappearing nations by a rising sea level and increasing regularity of diseases is for real. It is disturbing enough to shake us out of our slumber and instill a mission-mode readiness in our efforts. A determined global effort is needed to shift to the use of renewable energy regime. An environment friendly and sustainable regime is needed which will not add burden on the future generations for our deeds.

The understanding requires the nations to inculcate a 'eco-eco' ideology, which calls for an 'ecology-economy' equilibrium. Sustainability does not come at the price of growth and development and human endeavor can deliver them simultaneously. They can coexist and enrich each other to the benefit of coming generations.

A major breakthrough in our efforts can happen only if we adopt attitudinal change. The mentality of 'robbers' loot has to give way for sharing of resources - whether land, water or minerals. Resources should become a perpetual tool and not exhaustible reserves if the development is pragmatic. Such efforts would require involvement of people at every stage of planning, execution and evaluation and paradigm shift is essential in our centrally dictated use of resources and sense of ownership could infuse miracles and bring about a turnaround in the conservation of resources for future generation.

With a sense of ownership, responsibility towards the use of resource will be generated. The tribal will be integrated into forest management and fishermen as coastal eco-force. While each citizen will develop energy efficient outlook, every farmer will take care to enrich fields. Participation of people will accelerate the pace of efforts which appear isolated and insufficient when planned by the authority.

This does not abdicate the state of its responsibility. It, rather, becomes more relevant and the crusade has to be carried proactively by the State. Promotion of energy efficient equipments, a gradual policy shift to renewable sources of energy and promotion of public transport systems in city have to be state's priority. The land resource sustenance has to be integrated with forest protection, conservation and promotion. Efforts like social and urban forestry have multifarious dimensions and transmit multiple gains to the society. Such programmes have to be integrated with the lives of the population by percolating them to the grassroots.

Sustainable agriculture could strengthen the backbone of weakening food security. Proper planning of land use with dedicated grazing fields, bio-fertilizers and manures, natural pests as pesticides and making each drop of irrigation water count can deliver better returns from our efforts to maintain the fertility of our land resources. The shift from demand based to region specific needs to be appreciated to develop each region holistically on its strength.

Industrial accountability is a key which can unlock the secret to humanity's survival. A more responsible behaviour from the profit mongers can be evinced by taxation or through the innovative approach of "natural resource accounting and budgeting". A monetary value to every careless act of polluting the natural resource may heighten the awareness of these growth seekers. Plantation can be promoted by industries as part of their social responsibility.

Proper waste management system for cities with planned landfills or incineration plants is a must as urbanization is the order of the day; sustainable cities can become gateways for a long term growth. Water harvesting through rooftop systems and pollution check of vehicles would ensure a greener environment and availability of water for future generations. Slums - which standout for their poor hygiene and irreverence towards ecology - must receive a holistic up gradation plan.

Yet another tool is Environment Impact Assessment, which should become a mandatory organ of any development scheme. It is an anticipatory and preventive effort, which utilizes multidisciplinary knowledge to predict and prevent the damages that development project may bring along. This tool would promote the simultaneous march of sustainability with ecology.

The lop sided approach of human march on this planet has raised issues of his own survival. It has been an act of hara-kiri. We have denounced 'common-sense' and 'rational' for the dictated and imposing. Development of the resources should be a democratic process for and by the people. Each region has unique variables and each should be strengthened to find its own sustainable solution. It calls for recognition of local, traditional and indigenous wisdom. It demands a "glocal" approach - where the vision is global but action at grassroots level is local.

The problem of securing a better future for coming generations is a genuine and real concern, where the onus is on each one of us. The effort has to come not only at global organizations, but through actions of every individual as we strive towards the Gandhian concept of Swaraj - the village republics. It is through small efforts at local levels that our resources will be sustained for a better tomorrow. 'A beautiful waterfall, a majestic tiger, lush green farms of paddy and cool breeze of spring' should remain a experience for generations to come and not reduced to pages from history. The mission has begun. Future beckons our sense of responsibility and we must stand and work for it.

# The Pursuit of Happiness

**"What is this life, so full of care?**

**We have no time to stand and stare."**

The poet manages to strike a chord instantly through these immortal lines as somewhere within, each of us can identify with the sentiments expressed in these lines. There is a mad rush on our beautiful planet. And all of us contribute to this madness. Everyone is busy chasing and so dedicatedly absorbed in the chase that at times becomes oblivious to the object of the chase itself. We shroud it under different garbs-needs, wants, desires, dreams and ambitions-forgetting the elementary essence of each pursuit: happiness.

Poets, philosophers, authors and intellectuals have burnt many a grey cells in effort to encapsulate this ever eluding concept of "happiness". The very subjectivity of the concept gives it myriad interpretations. Each interpretation charts an entirely different course for the follower. No living being would ever deny their craving for this entity called "happiness" and would agree that sum total of their efforts are directed to this end. But how many can claim to have achieved this target? Is it actually an "end" or rather a mirage which is ever inviting and ever alluring? Is this pursuit, which characterizes every life on this planet, an undecipherable segment of life or is it the life itself ?

The attempts to decode this pursuit of happiness have generated epic volumes of literature and varied schools of thought. Defining the ends of this chase itself becomes a daunting challenge. The journey from cradle to grave is often spent in efforts to "realize" and make happiness "happen". The concept of happiness cannot be isolated from the social milieu which lends it different interesting flavours. In fact, the chase is "flagged off" for a toddler by this society itself.

The sharp shrill cry of a new born is laden with purity. Unaware of the social conditioning awaiting his formative years, the child has an innate treasure of happiness. It is this blessing, which every individual arrives with, that gets lost in this journey of life. It is this source of true happiness - a pure soul - which gets draped by malice and negativities as the interactions in social set up increase. And then begins a society dictated pursuit of something which each individual had within himself. A pursuit where we keep linking happiness to different objects, goals, needs, desires, wants, events or ambitions and thereby involve ourselves in a meaningless chase.

As the child steps into the school, his first laboratory of social interaction, we begin to rob him of his blessing of being happy. Academic targets are set and happiness is caged. A student is conditioned to feel happy only in the event of proving his one up-man ship over his peers. Whether in sports or studies, victory is emphasized by parents and teachers, to the extent that happiness becomes inextricably linked to achievements. We try to give "social" meanings to the concept of happiness for a child. He is conditioned to feel happy only when he achieves something over his peers. From an individual soul based concept, happiness becomes a comparative society based notion. The celebrations are reserved for "victories" rather than learning and participation of the child. This sets in motion, the pursuit of happiness, which society deftly keeps linking to different goals a person must chase.

Step into adolescence and the play of hormones begins to define a different parameter for happiness. A sweet smile and a favourable nod hold the power to create flutter in a young heart. Happiness attempts to regain the individualistic flavour where each one sings to the rhythm of his own tune.

"Beauty lies in the eyes of beholder" and the pursuit of happiness reconnects each one to purity of his own soul through love. The positivity of this unconditional and unalloyed emotion has immense power to strike the deepest chords of human soul. It is the common factor which furnished true happiness to a child in mother's lap and to a grown up in the embrace of his soul mate. The positivity of this emotion attempts to define happiness in true sense. It lends serenity to the roughs of ocean and an essential pause to the wild pursuit. It reconnects one to the soul and this inward peep holds the key to everlasting happiness.

The state of "real" happiness emanates from very basic human values. These values, like love, care, sympathy, kindness or forgiveness have a strange power to enrich the soul with long lasting happiness. In ambiences loaded with such emotions, one feels the comfort of true happiness, without indulging in any kind of pursuit. One's family is such one affiliation which provides happiness a different dimension altogether. The comfort of not being scanned by judgmental eyes, the freedom to be oneself and unconditional love and support from family members keeps one happy at heart. One may go through plethora of human emotions while going through varied situations of life but the underlining happiness survives in presence of families' love, care and support.

Another similar pillar which can help us scale insurmountable mountains with ease is presence of true friends. Friendship is yet another relation, chosen by us and grown on premise of those sacred soul enriching values, which can impart unparalleled happiness. In company of best friends, one cherishes the resonance of thoughts and time simply glides away seamlessly in endless rounds of chats, jokes, giggles and experiences. This seemingly carefree banter allows us to talk to ourselves, unwind and works as a therapy for soul. During such interactions human spirit is unbound of any pretension and can fly unperturbed by social norms and diktats. This flight, unlike any pursuit, soars one to real happiness.

However, the madness catches up on the individual once again. Career and ambition become the social parameters to determine the quantum of happiness an individual is entitled to. We keep delaying the celebration of happiness in the process of indulging in next pursuit. The happiness of moments is neglected waiting for the "bigger" event. The pursuit links happiness to the next promotion, a bigger house, the next vacation, events like marriage and child birth, a better job or pay package, a better car or a better posting. The chase for "betterment" continues to delay the celebration of present moments. We keep delaying for eternity the realization of having reasons enough to be happy. We neglect, fret over or simply ignore zillions of happy moments, waiting for the next "notional" target set by our social conditioning.

We also keep changing the symbol for our happiness from one materialistic possession to another. Soon we miserably mistake our needs, want and desires as our means of attaining happiness. And the pursuit becomes menacing, pacy, fiendish and even fatal at times. Even before one realizes, this pursuit hollows out an individual, turns him into a machine, snubs his soul into silence and swallows up his entire life in no time. The targets get auto revised each time a possession is achieved. Like grains of sands, the notion of happiness keeps slipping out each time, from between the gaps of the fingers in a clenched fist attempting to grasp it.

Years roll by and the pursuit continues, only because we fail to recognize the happy moments and in the process forget the essence of being happy. Years of a lifetime should not be wasted in such pursuits. Goals, targets, needs, desires and ambitions all need to be pursued but not viewed as means of attaining happiness. In itself, pursuits have a positive quality of engagement. They help in evolving as an individual and identifying oneself. They present a parameter to gauge one's abilities and skills in any chosen domain. Pursuits act as fuels to a competitive mind and help in challenging oneself to bring out the best. These chases introduce us to our own potential and help in giving some positive direction to the outlet of energies. However, happiness goes beyond all this. It must be de-linked from being an "end" of such pursuits. It is a state of mind. It is a natural condition of spirit and soul.

Happiness is a condition one can be in even while pursuing the individual goals and targets. Depending on what we decide to chase as our object of "notional happiness", our personality and the course of our life gets a definitive direction accordingly. For Alexander, the expansion of territorial dominance became a pursuit granting him happiness while for Lincoln, the fight against oppression infused similar thrill and passion. For Mother Teresa, happiness lay in selfless service and gestures for the lesser privileged while Ramanujan derived supreme happiness in mind crunching numbers and equations. Happiness is not the end of any pursuit. Every chase simply becomes an experience for the individual, preserved and linked to memory, which can be unfolded and decoded to derive happiness at any later stage in life.

In the next phase of everyone's life, the notion of happiness finds a different connotation with the professional success of the individual. Often people manage to club their professional pursuits with personal passions and derive an inexplicable thrill in the process. At times this thrill is also able to surmount the demands and conditionings of the society. While a good teacher may derive happiness in seeing his efforts translate into good individuals, a lawyer's criterion for happiness may be defined by clinching arguments in favour of his client in the court room. A doctor's pursuit of happiness must be having satisfying pauses whenever he saves a patient's life or gets smile back on their faces post recovery from some disease. An administrator's efforts of delivering social justice through neat framing and execution of policies must grant him doses of happiness while for a professional sportsman, victory in a coveted event may define the pinnacle of happiness. The underlying denominator in all these instances of happiness is the satisfaction one derives from something one is passionate about. Creating a masterpiece on the canvas for an artist or penning some immortal lines for a poet is the satisfaction of a creative urge which delivers loads of happiness to the person.

All these instances of successful pursuit of one's profession or passion are immensely satisfying and undoubtedly make one happy. These moments of happiness must be cherished. But the "real happiness" must not be overlooked in the blinding lights of these "successes". The professional endeavors are only a part of one's life, not life itself. Hence the personal segment of happiness must complement the satisfaction granted by such professional feats. The professional success must be cherished but the happiness springing on such occasions is dependent on achievements or excellence. Does it mean that happiness is only entitled to the competing and winning individuals?

Happiness is not restricted to a few. It is an emotion that each one of us is entitled to and must utilize to the maximum. Professional success only grants fleeting moments of happiness. The moments are transitory because the adulations received make the pursuit more vigorous and the craving more intense. However, this is a craving for success, praise, recognition and social appreciation and not of happiness. This kind of happiness does not enrich the soul and hence remains a hollow one. Does it match heart rendering happiness one experiences on watching a rainbow after rains or the sun going down in lap of ocean or snowflakes dripping from the needle shaped pine leaves or an innocent smile of a toddler or an early morning chirping of birds? Can the pristine beauty of the soul stirring landscapes of valleys, lakes, rivers, deep oceans, peaks, glaciers, corals and deserts have any parallel? It is the connection with the bounties of nature which makes one wonder at the futility of material pursuits. The "real" happiness lies somewhere out there, to be experienced in lap of Mother Nature.

Even before one can celebrate such professional achievement, the next target begins to hover on the mind and the pursuit intensifies. The pursuit has actually lost the right track and derailed the entire process towards chase of a mirage. One begins chasing the pale shadow of "real" happiness and almost tragically often the entire life is spent in such off the track pursuits.

True happiness is never hostage to social acceptance or appreciation. It must derive strength from honest efforts and must have an individualistic flavour. It springs from a satisfied soul. For an individual who learns new skill or contributes to the society or improves positively in any domain, the growth as an individual must be the cause of real happiness. The efforts to make this earth a better place to live in or bringing smiles to the face of a lesser privileged person should effuse true happiness. It is this kind of happiness which nourishes the soul and strengthens the character of an individual. It emanates positivity which delivers immense strength to the individual to weather out the rough phases of life also. It is this happiness which must be sought, not outside but by diving deep within oneself. The treasure chest of happiness is locked within each one of us and one must unlock it before sands of time cover it with negativity.

# Role of Education **in Development**

**"Yet, all experience is an archway.
Through which gleams, that untraveled world,
Whose margin fades, forever and ever."**

For the souls taking refuge in education, the desire for growth has no boundaries. Above lines from 'Ulysses', highlight the thirst of minds which are willing to learn. Education is not a destination, but a journey to be cherished. It is an enriching path, not only in lives of individuals, but also chartering histories of nations and building strong foundations of development.

In a developing society like ours, where an entire generation stands at crossroads of traditional values and western education, it becomes essential to define the parameters of education. For a traditionally rich country like ours, the roots of education can be traced back to compilation of Vedas. British furthered the cause of education in India. Though they introduced the study of English language to meet their administrative needs; it opened up a new world for Indians. It provided us with an opportunity to question - our beliefs, our customs and our knowledge and with that questioning, the spirit of education dawned.

Education has provided light of survival to several nations. Europe could march to development only after Renaissance. Indians could question the evils of sati and caste system only when reformers were exposed to ideas from western world. Even our freedom movement received impetus when we awoke to ideas of liberty, equality and fraternity from American and French revolutions. Though we could successfully overthrow the Britishers, their education system was adopted without questioning. Every society needs to reform the systems to meet some specific needs. However, the colonial education system has left a lot to be desired.

Education is an overall process of not only personal growth but an enriching growth of society and nation. It is the foundation of development of any nation. Educated youth have the ability to think beyond their stagnating lives and contribute to the development of their societies. Education arms individuals with the knowledge of their rights and duties. It is informed citizenry which forms the base for the development of any society.

Though the share in GDP may not reflect this reality, we have primarily been an agricultural economy. India still lives in its villages. The seeds of education must find their way to villages. The 'Adult Education Programme' and 'National Rural Education Programme' still have long distance to cover. By opening more primary schools in villages, we can not only curb the problem of migration by creating novel opportunities in village, but also educate farmers on knowledge of right seeds and fertilizers. This may lead to better yield and could again push back, the import of wheat and other essential commodities.

The quality of education needs better monitoring in both rural and urban India. Problems of teacher absenteeism in the villages deserve better scrutiny and punitive measures to ensure that children gain sufficiently from the time spent in school compounds. Awareness programs for girl child education must be carried out with more zeal and vigour.

Along with driving self-sufficiency education provides awareness. This awareness about the rights creates responsible citizens and responsible citizens can demand responsible and accountable governance. Education in field of IT has opened galaxy of opportunities in urban India with jobs in software, call centres and BPO's ushering in a revolution of sorts. The services sector, in this backdrop, is proving a significant contributor to the growth of economy. This knowledge hub has attracted large investments from several countries. The emphasis of government on technical education also highlights the commitment to drive excellence in areas of research and manufacturing.

Education plays a critical role in the democratic set up where an educated voter can make an informed choice. The voice of ballots gets translated into the fate of the voters through the levels of governance delivered. The policies charting the course of development of society get their nod from the representatives of people. Roads, ports, telecom, irrigation, industries, agriculture all demand simultaneous attention for a wholesome and inclusive development. Targeted policies in all these sectors must perform in unison for a balanced development to occur.

More number of higher universities will create a breed of individuals who are capable to chart their future in a growing economy. Education gives a level of confidence which capacitates individuals to compete globally and assert them. Such individuals become national asset with their contribution to the growth story of the nation. Through the entrepreneurial spirit they are able to create jobs and set up corporate empires to employ people. This employment generation goes a long way in raising the quality of life of several families. It is, thus, a positive spread effect which became possible from the seeds of education.

Growth generated by a robust economy has to be translated in overall rising of the standards of people. Often, the fruits of growth fail to reach the bottom of the pyramid. Such accumulation of wealth with few individuals has led to wide gulfs in the society. This trend is alarming and unhealthy for long term sustenance of the system.

This balancing of wealth in the society can occur when people imbibe the importance of education to change their fortunes. Education is that vital enabler which can move masses up the social ladder. It helps in upward mobilization of large segments of people who understand its importance and take the rightful refuge.

A holistic development of society is only said to occur when the material wealth is complemented by cultural, social and educational achievements. These are reflected in art, architecture, music, writings and the heritage of that society. All great civilizations of the world, which are remembered as developed, had attained that zenith on basis of importance accorded to education in those societies. The Romans, the Egyptians or closer home Magadha or Indus Valley boasted of rich lineage of scholars and universities which built a solid intellectual foundation and a progressive outlook for the society.

Education teaches manner to conduct the way of life which contributes to quality and standard of the individuals. Rich empires may rise and fall in a stroke but those with firm rooted educational groundings have an element of sustainability. This ensures their survival for ages. They derive their vitality from the rich corpus of knowledge, which guides them in survival, even during times of crisis. This knowledge bank, built on educational mantle, enriches the quest for development in such societies.

Education not only provides an opportunity for development in numerous spheres but contributes to the standard of living. Education of our culture and values should not take a back seat in this era of modernization.

For a holistic development, we must encourage at all levels an understanding of our tradition as part of our education. The effectiveness of this can be seen in people to people contacts with our neighboring country, which help us to enhance our international relations.

In this era of globalization, we may be tempted to neglect the fundamental. As a nation, we can't afford to do this at this junction. Education should remain the focus of government, ahead of their political agendas. Not only more policies but their effective implementation is essential in letter and spirit. Some modifications in our educational system is required to encourage talent based and growth oriented teachings. This would be a welcome step. Education for all should be the primary focus as it is the only gateway for sustained development and all round progress of our nation.

# Vision for Food Security in India

In pre-independence India, a rumble of dark clouds in the monsoon sky would enthuse the farmer with hope - a hope that his children will not have to sleep empty stomach for long in a chained nation. As the tryst with destiny began and the chains of oppression were shackled, the golden sparrow spread its' wings for a liberating flight. Dream of independence was studded with hopes - hope of emancipation from clutches of evils, hope of inclusive development and hope for a better quality of life for every individual. Though the grains of sand flowed down the glass hour, the Indian farmer still waits with bated breath for the rumbling of monsoon clouds. He waits patiently for timely downpour as clouds sail past the fields behind the shining nation's high-rises in close proximity to the fields. His children will still sleep hungry stomachs. Food security in India remains hostage to a number of factors. The promise of "food security" for all segments of Indian society still finds presence in the election manifestos of political parties.

Food-the most elementary need of any human being, has always been promised to the segment at the bottom of societal pyramid. Yet food security remains a distant dream in our nation. The visionaries paint a picture of a society where every individual enjoys guaranteed two meals per day of nourishing diet irrespective of his financial status. In such a society, the dreaded poverty line must have significance in terms of variations experienced in food grain availability. The vision is painted by a brush of hopes and hues of fruitful efforts. Somewhere the efforts to make this vision happen have lacked a vigor and direction. This path correction would pave way for attaining food security in our nation.

The roots of the problem can be traced to inability of food production to keep pace with the rate of increase in mouths to be fed. As limitation of horizontal spread of agricultural areas was felt in a nation were urbanization and industrialization is swallowing fields, the emphasis on enhancing vertical productivity and diversification to other food avenues was not carried out in a holistic manner.

Green revolution struck fantasy of this newly independent nation as a miraculous effort to obviate the agricultural woes. The combination of inputs in form of a package approach yielded unexpected results. High Yielding Variety (HYV) of seeds, irrigation facilities, fertilizers, pesticides and entrepreneurial spirit of a segment of nation's farmers demonstrated the result of collaborated efforts. However, the positivity was lost over time. Neither could the success be replicated in other crops and regions, nor could the region of focus deliver at the same levels of productivity. The surge in food production could not carry on indefinitely and soon stagnation in food production became a big question mark staring at the policy framers of this nation.

For the vision of food security to materialize, land reforms must find their place of priority. The ceiling laws were never applied legally on ground level. The powerful and influential continued their hold on large chunk of lands in names of different family members, resulting in depravation of land and associated oppression of lakhs of landless laborers. Even with a small landholding, the person would have managed to carry out sustenance agriculture for him and the family. This lot has thus been robbed of an opportunity of being food secure by improper compliance of ceiling laws.

Along with application of ceiling limits on land, its consolidation will also play a critical role in improving the net productivity compared to the same set as scattered landholdings. The economy of scale works in favour of consolidated landholdings as mechanization and expenditure on inputs would become a gainful venture in such scenario. No political party displays will to take onus of bringing about land consolidation and thereby contribute in direction of food security. The litigations at ground level and conflicting interests of appeasement prevent any such step from seeing light of the day. The fear of disputes regarding location of consolidated land and ownership issues vitiating the village harmony prevents any proactive effort in this domain. This hampers the mechanization of farming in major agricultural belts dominated by small and marginal landholdings.

The vision of food security demands concerted planning of agriculture in accordance with the agro-climatic zones of the nation. Each zone must cater to its strength and make the best use of its resources. Each zone would require a dedicated team comprising of motley of experts - from agro scientists, geologists, geographers, crop scientists, economists, soil scientists, to policy framers, implementers and the farmer - to plan in a holistic and sustainable manner for the region. The planning must also take into account the effect of global warming and climate changes on that particular zone and should be periodically revised to that effect. Each zonal plan must reflect the sensitivities about the weather, nature of soil, nature of suitable inputs, average size of landholdings and the financial condition of landowners of the region.

Unavailability of sufficient and timely credit is a big roadblock in getting the farmers their due. Deeper percolation of credit delivery system would ensure that farmers prevent the clutches of high interest rate charging local moneylenders of the region. Farm suicides in Vidarbha is testimony to the extreme steps that destructs families once the farmer is caught in the vicious debt trap in absence of a strong and reliable credit delivery system.

Soil testing and guidance forms another critical domain to promote food security in the nation. Soil scientists and laboratories must play a proactive role in reaching out to the farmers of their zone with inputs and crop related advice. Nature of soil is the guiding factor in deciding the type of suitable crop, number of crop rotations required and the choice of fertilizers and pesticides. The post harvest measures also demand heightened attention as these losses cause huge economical damage to a farmer, who has taken all right steps from seed to crop. Better approach roads, cold storage facilities, knowledge of market rates and a suitable Minimum Support Price (MSP) will guarantee farmers of a just amount for their farm products.

Another crucial input to improve productivity of crops is the timely and sufficient availability of water for the crops. Different crops require different dose of water and influence the choice of crops in the region. Irrigation means must make each drop of water count and contribute to the cause of improving food security of the nation. The use of dip and sprinkler irrigation techniques, highlighting the economy of each water drop, have enormously increased crop productivity in several regions of the nation. Regulating the use of pumps which damage the ground water levels and making positive efforts for recharging the water table are essential to introduce sustainability in our efforts. Creating small reservoirs or "a pond in each farm" concept must be promoted as an effective strategy for water conservation. De-silting of canals must be done regularly to ensure smooth flow of sufficient water in these lifelines for crops. Insulating crop productivity from uncertainty in monsoonal rainfall, saving "each drop as it falls" for judicious and effective use is indispensable.

Sustainability must also find reflection in our efforts by calibrating use of synthetic fertilizers and pesticides along with the green alternatives. Active adoption of Integrated Pest Management (IPM) and Integrated Water

Management (IWM) methodologies will yield holistic results and ensure sustainability of resources. This guarding of depletion of resources by measuring each action of our generation with an eye on future is paramount. Integration of biological and traditional means along with the suitable nutrient enriched fertilizer for the soil would ascertain richer dividends for many generations to come.

The concept of food security for every individual nation will materialize only when diversification of food occurs beyond the agricultural products. Each region will have to focus on its specific food basket. The ingredients must be sourced from horticulture, pisciculture, poultry and dairy farming. Coastal regions and stretches of inland fishing must incentivize the fishing communities. Use of environment friendly mechanized means would increase the yield of catch for the fishermen, get them more money and improve chances of food security of them and their families. Also the food from these varied fields would substitute the conventional demand and reduce pressure on production from land based sources.

Introduction of region specific cash crop as part of rotating crops in field will boost the net economic returns from same field. With little credit support from the banking system, poultry or dairy activity can be pursued by entrepreneurial farmers to supplement their field incomes. Such initiatives must be encouraged in every region to recreate the magic of "white revolution", which brought prosperity and food security to a large segment. Development of community owned orchards on the Gram Sabha lands can contribute to additional income of farmers of the village. Apart from providing additional income to the farmers, such diversification ventures would also contribute to the nutritional requirements of citizens. The sordid tale of malnutrition in several pockets of our nation being worse than sub-Saharan Africa is no longer a hidden secret. To fight such alarming levels of nutritional deficiency, immediate steps to promote diversification of agriculture must be taken up on mission mode urgency.

Developing each agro-climatic zone in a wholesome manner is essential for ensuring food security of the nation. Coarse grains have been left on the margins of attention by researchers. The vision of food security will translate into reality once the over reliance on rain fed agriculture culminates and each zone develops self sufficiency in food basket. Dry land regions must lead the drive and diminish their dependence on rain fed agricultural tracts. Research to improve productivity and discover better strains of maize, sorghum, jowar, ragi, pulses and millets would boost their production and benefit large tracts of the nation where the major crop. With a high nutritional content, sustained focus and assistance to farmers of these crops can deliver an "evergreen revolution" for the dry zones of the nation.

The technique of crop rotation must be judiciously employed in each region in consultation with the soil scientists and agricultural universities of the region. More field visits and interactive modules for the agricultural students and intensive "lab to land" approach would benefit the productivity by transfer of knowledge. With the preparedness for climatic changes in each agricultural zone intensifying, the need for research and introduction of genetically modified crops would be vital in improving productivity. Climate change is a reality and we are standing on the brink of a catastrophe. The erratic cycle of rainfall, extremes of temperatures, storms, cyclones and submerging coastlines would alter the growth and maturity cycles of several crops and this poses a climatic threat to the concern about food security. Resistant and fast maturing strains will have to be developed in response to survive the onslaught of climatic change.

It is ironical that the vision for food security in a primarily agricultural nation seems farfetched and distant from reality. It demands concerted effort from all the stakeholders. But food security could still elude millions till the access to food grains is simplified and freed from the clutches of a corrupt and creaking distribution system. Even with better economic returns from their fields, a farmer may not be able to afford the prevailing market prices of food products. Thus, despite increasing productivity and diversification of agriculture, the vision of food security may still be blurred. How do we then cleanse the debilitated distribution machinery to make this increased production reach the right beneficiaries at an affordable price?

The ills of the Public Distribution System in our nation are too many to be enumerated. The system has almost lost its purpose and utility for the deserving and has collapsed in face of vested interests, weak monitoring and abundant leakages. Right from selection of beneficiaries to the movement of grains, transparency and accountability is found wanting. The alternative approach of Direct Benefit Transfer whereby the bank accounts of the beneficiaries are linked for transfer of subsidy offers a glimmer of hope. The biometric backdrop of this initiative might prove to be a game changer in reducing the stronghold of powerful and influential in beneficiary selection at the village level. Though a lot of groundwork still needs to be done, transfer of subsidy amount straight away to accounts of beneficiaries will help them gain access to the food available in the market.

For a nation claiming the mantle of global leadership, the vision for food security must be translated into reality at the earliest. It is also linked strongly with the livelihood security of the citizens, which when realized would capacitate them with financial strength to approach the market. Better schemes for generating self and wage employments would empower individuals financially. The norms for deciding the levels of subsidy will have to be re-thought and linked to the index of inflation. This would address the gap between an individual's income and the level required to ensure food security in market. All efforts to contain the galloping food inflation will have to be put in place. Strict monitoring and regulation of spot trading, hoarding and cartelization must be carried out by authorities with vigilance and transparency. These and several other measures proposed have been floating in domains of discussion forums, political promises and implementation manuals for too long a time now. It is time they are drawn out and their potential realized. Their cumulative application would result in enhanced food productivity, better economic returns and easier access to food grains in market for one and all. Only after putting the worry of sustenance behind, would the efforts for greater growth and quality of life crystallize. The security cover is comforting, rejuvenating and motivating for any individual. With the assurance of his family getting sufficient nutritional food, his performance in his endeavors would multiply. Such efforts would bring positive developments and prosperity for one and all.

# **Social** Networking

**"What is this life, so full of care?**
**We have no time, to stand and stare."**

The poet encapsulates the futility of our continuous struggle for survival in this world of cut-throat competition. In spite of the consensus that the most beautiful and worthy pleasures for human existence are for free, the rat race for materialistic pursuit inevitably drags us all. As constraints of time crept in to limit the social involvement of individuals, concerns about this diminishing human network and increasing isolation became bolder. Technology tried to rescue humanity by providing a platform- a virtual alternative for a real problem. But has the solution managed to simplify or added to the complexities of social networking?

As a social animal, the need to communicate and share has been an intrinsic part of human beings. The evolution from nomadic existence to settling in a societal relationship provided a much desired stability to human life form. Sharing of joys, sorrows, fears, anxieties, thoughts and ideas amongst the individuals in neighborhood lent beauty to human social existence. Celebrations of fairs and festivals in a common festive spirit enveloping the neighborhood reflected the bonhomie springing from the "real" social networking.

The pace of change in lifestyles has been rapid over the past few decades. The lively neighborhood chats, the leisurely evening strolls and sharing of tales with neighbors for un-ending hours appear as post retirement indulgences. The cut throat competition for grades in schools, deadlines for submissions of projects in colleges and the need to professionally outsmart others to survive leaves us bereft of time to enjoy the simple pleasures of sharing in a social milieu.

The advent of internet and information technology, however, presented a new dimension to the social networking phenomenon. With traditional communication methods failing to keep pace with demands of instant communication, several new platforms for exchange emerged in the virtual world. From use of pigeons, telegrams and fax communication leapfrogged into an era of e-mail and internet messengers. With technology as a facilitator, distances were diminishing.

E-mails soon became a medium for exchange of views, thoughts and information globally within the wink of an eyelid. Business gained immensely as vast amount of data could be exchanged globally without any time lag. The platform was also cost-effective when compared to the existing telecommunication scenario. Though it gave a big boost to social connectivity, a bigger platform was yet to emerge.

The last decade has witnessed growth and proliferation of the social networking sites, providing a virtual world to connect with people globally. MySpace, LinkedIn, OpenBC, Orkut and FaceBook have become integral part of lives of most net using community. These sites provide a platform for user to create a profile and quench the very fundamental need of human existence-the social connectivity.

A profile creation on these sites is first step towards entering a virtual world of opportunities. It enables one to search for friends, acquaintances, relatives, teachers, employers and anyone globally and remain "in touch" with the person. Sharing of views, thoughts, ideas, data and pictures has been facilitated by regular updates. School and college farewells are no more final goodbyes to the classrooms as the virtual connectivity fills in for the real absence of those friends. People have discovered lost friends and made several new ones in their ever-expanding friend list on such sites.

Tremendous popularity of these sites is evident form the result of several surveys amongst the net users, which vouch for considerable time spent on these sites for "connecting". The phenomenon which grew in form of groups discussing common interest or affiliated to same alma mater became open for all subsequently. Though most popular amongst youth and teenagers, even the parents are finding it increasingly useful to relive nostalgia by connecting with their childhood friends or being "friend" of their child on internet.

Social networking in virtual medium has refocused on the basic need of an individual to connect to people and share. Simple human tendencies were getting lost in the humdrum of a pacy struggle of survival. The viral nature of expansion of membership indicates a desire to seek belongingness in the members of present society. These sites, with their impersonal nature of communication, also provide flexibility to the individual to escape any uncomfortable conversation at a single click.

Social networking in virtual medium can be immensely helpful in widening domains of tastes and knowledge. While real networking on face to face basis may not provide one with opportunities to make friends globally, these sites draw down the gender, region, linguistic or other boundaries. This also helps in downplaying any apprehension and prejudices one may carry in making a new approach. This networking aids the knowledge of diverse cultures, music, foods, languages and traditions. Friends from different parts of the globe can share the distinctiveness of their part of the world through views and pictures.

Another advantage of breaking barriers in a connected world is enrichment from experts. Groups and communities formed on these sites around a common hobby or interest can be highly rewarding for the members. The exchange of ideas and details about the pursuit is an excellent means to further one's interest in the field. Advice and counseling from experts in that domain proves invaluable bonus, which may not have materialized through a real face to face networking.

Social networking in a virtual world also provides a platform to showcase one's talent globally. Many videos of talented singers, dancers, instrumentalists aspiring for a breakthrough are uploaded regularly on You-tube. They all might not manage to eye catch any mentor, yet with increasing "views" of the video, will bestow happiness of appreciation and recognition, which is priceless for any artist.

In a day to day interaction, these sites provide a useful medium to share information with multiple contacts. Changes in ones' contact phone number, correspondence address or a job switch can be intimated to all by a single posting on these sites. Batch parties can be coordinated and venue, date, timing can all be conveniently "posted" to all concerned. Whether an alumnus meet or a farewell party, the "virtual" world facilitates easy notification for people to gather in "real" scenarios.

The virtual world based social networks have proved immensely useful in reaching out to larger people in case of emergencies and disasters. Several administrators have off-late used social networking platforms to contact agencies for relief and rescue measures. A stage of emergency management, mitigation, preparedness, response and recovery have simplified due to backbone of the networking tool. A single message can be relayed and passed to multiple users to arrange for a required blood group in scenarios where real life communications face constraints of limited reach. Delhi Police has been constructively using Facebook page to publicize about notorious elements and eliciting community help. Information about vital places like ATMs, blood banks, hospitals, schools, collectorate office can be obtained from any person of that city by simply posting the query on their "wall". Social networking on internet, due to wide reach, has potential to formulate and circulate opinions in a vibrant civil society.

The Arab Spring demonstrated this potential to the fullest as the entire region erupted in a pro-democracy mood. Videos and pictures of heavy handedness of the regime splashed on the social networking sires exposed the brutality and united the emotions of people. It also provided a medium to plan marches, venues and timings when physical contact amongst the protestors was restricted by the regime. The power of masses could be displayed on "real" streets but the medium which managed this "real" revolution remained a "virtual" one.

The pictures posted on these sites have also led to several unfathomable revelations. The open availability of some of these messages and pictures has helped many authorities to understand realities, which could have been conveniently brushed under the carpet. At times, parents and principal have uncovered lies of their wards about partying or alcoholism through the uploaded accessible pictures. At other instances, police has managed to catch criminal gangs by discussion of their modus operandi or tracked missing people by describing them to "real" people on this "virtual" medium. Employers have snooped in to find employees bunking offices on pretext of emergency at other place or sharing unacceptable views about the organization. Thus, access and transparency have increased manifold often to the inconvenience of many.

Like every other tool of technology, social networking in virtual space has its dark angles. The activities involving tabbing at computer keys to generate responses and variation on screen have been found to be addictive for many youngsters. The addictive behavior is not only consuming their precious time but also producing disastrous consequences at times. Networking through a virtual platform presents one with anonymity to present only one aspect of our personality. The pictures splashed on the sites and the messages are selectively relayed to create an image which is "like-able" and "acceptable" to larger society. It is a form of escapism from oneself and realities of one's life by displaying a "happening" image of one. Addicts can hardly wait for an event to finish or new dress to be purchased before splashing them online to garner positive comments. Favourable comments are waited for and much time is lost in peeping into insignificant events in lives of people who hardly matter but shine on our profiles as "friends".

The time devoted by an individual in isolation tabbing away at keyboard for social activity could have been creatively used to pursue a hobby or interest, contributing to the growth of an individual. This entire duration of virtual connectivity disconnects him from his "real" surroundings and "real" people. The participation level in real world activities diminish and concern for family, friends and other face to face relationships decreases. While the person manages to stay "in-touch" and reduces distances with a geographically distant friend, often the distances between his real close ones sitting next to him increase tremendously.

The present day trend of networking has also raised concern about a slew of mental health related issues. Intense use of this medium has been generating focusing or concentration problems for the youth. The virtual environment conditions the individual for small attention span as he gets accustomed to quick instant responses from his friends. Also, as the person simultaneously "handles" multiple chats, his focus for a particular response is sufficiently low. The quality of talks is also superficial and often lacks gravity, laced with emotions, as found in face to face interactions. This leads to problems in adjusting to real people and their responses in the real world with the person showing irritable impatience. Psychologists also point out that such "addicted" behavior displays "a need of constant reassurance" that they exist. Other manifestations emerge in form of worsened communication skills with difficulty of articulation of thoughts into proper words. The virtual networking involves quick commenting and use of emoticons (emotion displaying icons) which effects the growth of proper word usage and spell sense.

Addictive involvement in virtual social network cuts the individual away from reality. The interest in pursuits like games and shopping is also decreased as even these interests are satisfied through online ventures on related sites. Another issue causing concern relates to poor judgment capability of the teenagers in selecting online friends. Bullying or harassment by posting threat messages, publicizing private messages or embarrassing pictures or spreading rumors has caused bouts of avoidable anxiety and depression amongst teenagers.

Such bullying incidents, with associated ignominious humiliation, have also led youth to extreme steps of taking their own lives. Cases of sexual advancements by pedophiles who pose as teens and lure youngsters into real world contact have sent shivers down the spines of users who treat this as an innocuous medium. Researchers have shown that lack of face to face network could alter the way genes perform, upset the immune responses, hormone levels, functioning of arteries and influence mental performances which causes increased risk of health problems as cancer, stroke, heart diseases and dementia, along with undermining social skills and ability to read body language.

Virtual social networking sites, not only provide medium for communication but also provides opportunity for extension of one's personality into virtual world by asking one to disclose their hobbies, gender, likes, dislikes, educational and professional backgrounds. Often fake profiles are created to portray a desired image or trick people into eliciting information.

Such networks have also helped offices to expand business through wide circle of contacts and spend less on advertising by giving them marketing opportunities at a low cost. However, employees indulging in such networking during office hours have raised concern about decreased productivity. Hackers also target social networking sites as they can commit frauds or launch malware attacks. They have also indulged in data or identity theft by asking for personal details. The third party applications on FaceBook may not be totally safe. Some have potential to be used to infect computers with malicious codes which can be used to collect data from the user's site.

Like any other product of human creation, internet and virtual networking has its own share of pros and cons. Many a times, the awareness of "privacy settings" to prevent identity theft or theft of personal information is missing, which is used to commit frauds or shopping in other persons' account. In this commercial world and materialistic lifestyles, social networking is essential but the virtual can never replace the warmth of real networking. The scarcity of time cannot force one to substitute virtual for real. The joy of shared smiles, the enthusiasm of articulating thoughts with laced emotions, contortions of face and movement of hands along with interjecting the loved ones' narratives to put one's own additions has its own irreplaceable charm. Virtual world has diminished distances and enhanced the number of people in our friend list. But are they "all" really our "any-time" depending source we can turn to in distress? Can a beaming voice of "Happy New Year" by replaced by scribbling the same on the profile of your loved one? Can a comforting hands' touch or shoulder to cry on be replaced by widening virtual contacts? Networking in virtual world has helped us maintain links with people and improved access to a wider world at our fingertips; however it demands moderation as a healthier alternative to enable people to derive the best of the benefits it can deliver.

# Globalization and WTO
## An Era of Neo-imperialism

**"Arise, awake and stop not till the goal is reached."**

This clarion call by Swami Vivekananda resonates with relevance, for citizens and leaders of this nation, reminding them of the momentous occasion in the journey. The 'tryst with destiny' has reached a critical junction. We – as a nation – have arrived on the global stage. Though the journey had its share of hardships and pitfalls, we managed to emerge with élan. And now is the time to showcase our strength, through confidence in dealing with global institutions, putting the haunting imageries of imperialism to deepest of graves.

Imperialism was a curse on our nation - sapping our diversity and richness in all possible ways. It left us economically hollows, politically fragile and morally impoverished. It was a burden. The scars of which, left a deep impact on the fabric of Indian society. The recovery took time - but the prolonged process of recovery has ensured that it is sustainable.

As an independent nation, dealing with myriad of problems - illiteracy, malnutrition, lack of infrastructure - India chose to do its own experiments and learn from them. We evolved, nurturing the sectors of our economy, till we had the confidence to open up and compete. India built its strength and rode through the era of 'Hindu growth rate' before opening up our economy to winds of globalization.

Discarding the 'frog in the well' mentality, India decided to face the global forces face -on. A bold step in realm of economics was about to usher in a revolution in the history of the nation. The forces of global integration touched all spheres of human existence social, cultural, political.

The era of protectionism gave way to era of competition. Both the lethargy stuffed public sector and the nurtured small scale industries faced the heat of competition under the new industrial policy. Competition, though uneven, was call of the day. With adequate support from the government, began a reform - a movement to drive in efficiency and strength into the Indian industries. Globalization exposed our firms to cutting-edge technologies and methodologies for adoption.

The global forces struck back the fear of British industries, which sapped our raw materials and ruined our cottage industries. Fears of neo-imperialism are not misplaced. However, the context has changed. The playground is different and the turf is to our favour. The availability of less costly foreign goods might hamper certain industries but it is here that the democracy unleashes its strength, through a government committed to protect the interest of its citizens. Imperialism had a political backing which radiated exploitation of colonies but now the rules are ours. As a sovereign nation, the market forces are not dictated upon but regulated enough to ensure equity.

The global presence has strengthened the role of governance, which has rolled back from some sectors to allow market to serve people better, but not vanished from these arenas. Through efficient regulation, it ensures the ethos of socialism is not diluted. Consumerism, a by-product of global forces, may accentuate the class cleavage but the state ensures that the growth is inclusive by adequate intervention.

Globalization also presents us with opportunities to display our strengths on the global arena. The inequity in distribution of resources led to the emergence of strength based economies. As the societies evolved and barter of commodities proved insufficient to meet needs of all, an organized manner of trade began. Soon, the need to have a platform for negotiations and dispute resolution arose and the birth of World Trade Organization (WTO) arranged. Global trade was better regulated to prevent distributions and exploitation of weaker by dominant.

Trade has become the backbone of present day growth and prosperity of nations playing a crucial role in maintaining the foreign reserves and in fulfilling the deficient resource; it has multifarious impact on the destiny of the nation. However, the arena of trade is also one of incessant negotiations and discussions as our nation wishes to gain. The conflict assumes giant dimensions when the issue is not quantum of gain, but rather a profit-livelihood tussle.

WTO - as a democratic platform has provided an arena for developed and developing nations to settle the long stretched issue, the infamous Doha round. The high agricultural and export subsidies provided by developed nations, make their products cheaper, than the cost intensive products by the developing nations. This tilts the scale in favour of the cash rich nations even in agriculture - the mainstay for the developing nations like ours. To prevent the onslaught of these subsidized products to our markets, the high tariff rates stand justified.

The WTO stand-off and other similar negotiations have offered a platform to put forward and be resolute upon our demands, even in face of pressure. For nation like ours, it is the matter of livelihood of millions of farmers, involved in subsistence agricultural and it cannot be sacrificed at the altar of global trade. The resolute unflinching stand is a reflection of 'our' commitment to the welfare of 'our' farmers; a reflection of holding ground against winds of globalization; an indication of our arrival on global front.

The pressures brought by globalization may appear to be imperialistic, but rather they are modern day challenges for the society and governance. This is an age of 'global village', where challenges will be multidimensional, but they can be squeezed to our favour by skill in dealing with them.

The integration of society exposed us to different cultures lifestyles, food, music and dances of the world. This may attain imperialistic contours, once we start a blatant imitation of these aspects. They all evolved in a society and reflect the traits of those societies. And also is the diverse treasure of our music, food, dances. The need is to recognize and value our strengths, than be overawed by anything foreign.

British imperialism could wreck our culture by eliminating the patronage it received. It could threaten the integrity as the concept of nation had not evolved. A tumultuous freedom struggle and sixty years of independent nationhood has given us an immense confidence as a nation-with no fears of disintegration and subjugation. Neo-imperialism should not even have strength to raise an eye against the mighty strength that India, as a nation possesses.

The global donations for various social issues and governance matters often have an economic undertaking. They often enforce 'democracy' as an instrument to fulfill the latent economic aims. The prescription is parochial and through tinted glasses they fail to value the local conditions.

'Unique situations demand unique solutions'. Solutions which are home grown, which reflect local wisdoms and skills to handle the problem. The governance should step up to promote such culture of decentralized decision making units, rather than implanting a dictated plan. The forces of globalization must be handled and their arena defined, upholding holistic growth as a priority.

The forces generated by our global integration should propel our growth story. Through mergers and acquisitions, our businesses can play a better role in global domain. Global technology can help unlock our resources for regional development. Whether as collaborations to set up Public Sector Units or the recent oil exploration in Barmer by Cairns, the positivity of global strength must be tapped. The assistance by Japanese in cleaning plan for Yamuna, the collaboration with Koreans for Delhi Metro or the active role played by civil society organizations like Greenpeace have highlighted a positive and confident approach to handle foreign funds and agencies.

An era of neo-imperialism may fail to dawn if the strength of nation is adequate to thwart any such design. In profit oriented dealings of the day, genuine welfare may be a rarity. Global forces will seek profit, but to curb this need from metamorphosing into greed, the role of state is crucial. The state must remain true to its commitments towards citizen and use platforms like WTO for better gains on basis of strength of economy.

As a potential superpower, India should exude such confidence and dispel any aspersions about neo-imperialism arresting its success. A "glocal" approach is the call of the day, where the vision is global but approaches local. Such small steps will build capacity of the country to overcome internal challenges and resist global pressures. Globalization presents opportunities. It is like an orchard, where fruits abound and can be gathered by tiptoeing around the thorns. The vehicle of globalization should be used to create the destination of Gandhian Swaraj and ensure rise of one and all.

# Gender Equality
## A Myth or Reality

Humans have often contorted religious texts and misinterpreted them to meet their selfish desires. In such misdeeds, lies the misfortune of women of India. Women - the originator of life who deserved respect and rights were subject of numerous atrocities, right from the medieval era. Evil practices like sati and female infanticide trace to their origins to those pages of history. Unfortunately, though progress was made virtually in every sphere, as a nation we are still struggling with the problem of gender equality.

Gender equality seems like an ideal concept. A concept which we have seen being materialized in other nations but remains a mirage in a culturally rich nation like ours. It is a concept which emphasis on abilities of individual, rather than discriminating on the basis of gender. Our society promotes the concept of male domination by giving preference to boys right from childhood. We are yet struggling to shake off the concept of male being the breadwinner of family.

In families, riddled with economic constraints, having both girl and boy child, it is still prevalent to stress on education of the boy. The mobility from the rural regions is still limited. While the boy is easily sent to larger towns by parents, most parents are protective about sending their girl child to look for employment in bigger cities. They are confined to household chores or duties in the farms. The equality or even the notion of it is blown to winds.

The effort to bring about equality between rights and privileges to be enjoyed by genders meets stiff resistance from the societal set up. The prevalence of the dowry system is a major hurdle in efforts to bring this equality. Parents keep the girl devoid of any privileges, including investment in her education, as they plan for savings to be given at her time of marriage. This neglect in her own family is de-motivating and leads to a reduced levels of self confidence in the woman. Her potential is snubbed in all these formative years and ability to think freely and contribute ideas dwindle in an authoritarian male biased environment.

Times have changed tremendously whereby the progress of our nation is analyzed in backdrop of economy or growth. But we still remain rooted to past when representation is demanded by women. It has never been about ability but about chance, which was denied to potential performers in all fields which required the women to move out of the closets.

The alarming figures of female mortality rate and female foeticide can shake off the mask of globalization we demonstrate. These obnoxious acts are not confined to remotest of villages either where every malady can be blamed on lack of education. Surveys demonstrate that such acts are carried out vigorously in hearts of progressive metros of the nation with affluent and "modern" culprits. Easy availability of diagnostic facilities to unravel the gender of the child have been grossly misused in cities to carry out sex selective abortion by the rich and educated citizens of our nation. It boils down to the dark mindset behind those garish masks of modernity. Strict monitoring of such illegal centres and proper implementation of PNDT Act has also been lacking. Recent cases of sati from a village or reports of dowry deaths continue to plague the concept of gender equality.

Even in other spheres, though participation of women has increased, they have met increasing resistance from male dominated society. In politics, the women reservation bill is yet to see the light of the day in parliament. It has already generated much debate and controversy over an issue which women deserve as a right. Unless women are represented in sheer numbers in forums of influence, sensitivity towards the cause of women empowerment in policies, programs would be lacking. Male mindsets have been rigid and have blocked attempts by women to shackle the chains of subservience.

Lack of proper education still poses a challenge for the women in our nation. Though schools have been opened in villages and encouragement is being given through schemes like Sarva Shiksha Abhiyan and Mid Day Meal scheme, the enrolment ratio of girls still needs to pick up. More than the schemes, a proactive participation at Panchayat level and awareness of an educated girl child need to be stressed on. Reservation has ensured that a woman candidate gets elected from such seat but on the ground level, her voice is still stifled by the member of her own household. As a pawn, her name is used to win election and her voice of empowerment is silenced thereafter. She would hardly be seen in village meetings or in active decision making forums, which continue to be the male bastions. This situation needs legal and policy level support to deliver the real ethos behind such reservations.

Several steps have been taken through policies and programmes of government. We have moved in right direction but achieving gender equality is still a distant goal. The Domestic Violence Act is a step in right direction to empower women. Active programmes with incentives need to be introduced, especially in villages, to promote education amongst girls. Higher education avenues must be started in remote place to enable girls realize their potentials.

The institution of marriage must also be approached in slightly unconventional manner by the Indian society. There is need to move on from the traditional way of allocating fixed roles to the individuals entering this arrangement. The talented individuals must maintain their professional identity and need not sacrifice their potential to make this institution work. As partners, they must work out the most convenient manner of balancing family and work. Often, a sabbatical taken in default by the woman during child birth marks the end of her professional journey. This arrangement needs to change by adopting a flexible and adjusting approach, which gives space for both individuals to realize their fullest potential.

Even in cities, the society needs to evolve and create space for women on an equal platform. Incidents of violence against women in major cities highlight that the problem lies in correcting the male mindset than any other variable. This must be inculcated through sustained moral teaching of a male child in his formative years in the family. Also zero tolerance for crime against women should be brought in as measure of deterrence in the society. The offenders who get away with light or no punishment in such cases are emboldened and become threats to repeat such heinous and shameless acts. For gender equality to become a reality, effective implementation of harsh laws has to be done with zero tolerance for violation for a sustained period in a fire fighting manner.

Women have a crucial role to play in development of nation. In an era, when Kiran Desai, Sania Mirza and Joshna Chinappa are winning laurels for our country and leaders like Sheikh Hasina and Bachelette are running nations, gender equality needs to be imbibed in a practical manner. Gender equality may not be a reality in practice but it is a goal worth chasing. Every small step in this direction would be a milestone in empowering women with their due. Each small success would be a liberating and enriching experience-both for the individual and the nation. There is no dearth of policies, only willingness is needed on a national level to rise above petty and myopic notions, and implement them for an empowering cause. It is time for our nation to count for contributors in its quest for development and not allow gender inequality be a hurdle in the mission.

# Role of Media in Maintaining **Communal Harmony**

The values and ethos enshrined in the constitution have been the guiding force in making a path of stability and progress for the nation. The institutions deriving their vitality from these golden tenets and furthering this wisdom and philosophy into society maintain a healthy progressive balance. With the roll of time in this independent nation, the three pillars-executive, legislature and judiciary-have successfully shouldered the responsibility of navigation in troubled waters. Threat to sovereignty, deepening of democracy, promotion of inclusivity in every sphere of life or maintaining communal cohesiveness have all received at different times collaborative contributions from these wings of the Indian system. A fourth pillar has emerged over time to lend stability to the edifice and uphold the constitutional ethos and play a constructive part in the journey of nation building. The role of media- as this all pervasive force, expected to compliment the traditional structures cannot be undermined in the present day scenario.

This is an age of media's overpowering presence in every domain. As the accessibility to information simplifies, media manages to meet our senses through every other device. Diversifying from conventional sources of newspaper, magazines, television and radio, it now greets us through internet sites, billboards and mobile based ads. We are never too far from its all embracing presence. It is this reach which bestows media with a baggage of expectations and responsibility, in sensibly tackling the situations affecting the society at large.

Amongst several situations in the society where the role of media can be scrutinized and responsibility assigned, communal flare-ups remain a sensitive segment. The diversity and richness of threads weaving the fabric of Indian society forms the cause of it's' strength. The plurality of caste, colour, religion, language bestows us a unique set-up, rich with opportunities and challenges. In unity lies our strength, but we still have witnessed occasions where trivial situations have snowballed into major communal flare-ups.

The present day media is itself struggling on the crossroads of conflicting demands. The arena has expanded to promote competition between different brands-both in print and electronic media. The competition to attract eyeballs has recklessly clouded the fundamental role media was designed to perform. Often the ethics of responsible journalism are sacrificed at the altar, in bargain of sensationalism in reporting.

Communal flare-ups can be often traced back to some minor incident which could have been nipped in the bud. In contrast, they explode with evil repercussions, staining the smooth fabric of the society. Innocent lives are lost, families destroyed and properties ruined by invoking religious sentiments. Religion- the garb with the warmth of the same Almighty, albeit of different colours, is given a notorious interpretation and projected as the dividing wall on such occasions. The situation poses a challenge to the state machinery where each element has to work responsibly in restoring peace and order in minimal time to minimize the damage from the unmindful acts of perpetrators. Can media be abdicated from all responsibility in such an eventuality?

The free nation guarantees under Article 19 of Fundamental Acts, the freedom of expression, with media deriving its powers. But can the principle of self-restrain to deliver responsible reporting be discarded in the face of such challenges to the social harmony?

The power of media transmits the voices and images of riot struck families straight into our living rooms. With photographs of horror splashed across the front pages and bold lettering announcing the numerical record of the ghastly act, the coverage manages to transmit the fear and horror of the locality across geographical barrier. The flare-ups in one corner of the nation is dished out, often with inciting remarks, unaccountable figures and opinionated version of causes to every part of the nation. In a race to grab the eyeballs, the breaking news culture promotes the high speed transmission to acclaim being the first channel to beam the images of the horror. Often the research into the real cause of the outbreak is sidelined and the focus shifts to use of provocative language and promotion of blame game.

Irresponsible journalism ends up inflaming passions of community rather than highlighting the unmindful acts of few individuals. In such testing times, the media is expected to fulfill its role of fourth pillar in the system effectively and promote all possible measures to bring back calm and order in the society. Such times are the litmus test to judge the level of responsibility displayed by media in complementing authorities to normalize the situation.

An irresponsible reporting ends up making statements of gross generalization, demonizing an entire community for the pervert acts of a few. The words used-both by the print and electronic media-should be calibrated, measured and befitting the situation. A regulator for this purpose would face heavy resistance from media fraternity, but then these are the situations when self-regulation is put to real test.

Sensitive situations of communal flare-ups are often covered by novice reporters who skip the ground realities to indulge in self-investigated judgments and opinionated reporting. Often the personal biases of the reporter or the channel cloud the vision of the media, incapacitating it to present the objective realities of the situation.

Though large segment of Indian population has been swarmed by the availability of information, the discretion to dissect and analyze every news item is not a popular attribute. Most consumers in general and the rural population in particular, receive the news-piece on face value. Efforts are not made to scrutinize the report and decipher the finer unsaid elements. There is an implicit trust in media and the voice of the reporter carries enough weight for people at large. With its ability to highlight mis-governance and plight of the common man, media is seen as the voice of the masses. This rust has developed over years and hence the portrayal of any event by media makes a significant impact. The realty is seen through the lens of media. And this underlines the need of all the more sincerity and ethics in journalism in times of communal discord.

The curative role of media in maintaining communal harmony, post a communal event is immense. Steering away from any exaggeration or unmindful indulgence in blame game, media must confine itself to facts, without stressing on religious affiliations. The need of the hour is to invoke the humanity, which forms the base of all religions, rather than focus on the religious hues of the victims or perpetrators. Media can be the calming influence, working in tandem with the administration to bring a semblance of sanity back in the locality. It must relay the message of peaceful coexistence by broadcasting messages of reconciliation, brotherhood and harmony. Media must return to the basic of upholding national interest against any other narrow plausible gain while delivering its report.

Media's role in maintaining communal harmony is not linked to curative actions, but also has preventive aspects. All the ethos and values of constitution need to be continuously re-inforced amongst the population to enable them take incipient deep roots in the society. With its all pervasive coverage and continuous impact on almost entire population of the nation, media must promote peaceful coexistence between people of different region, religion and languages. It must promote seminars, debates and discussions bringing forth the richness of the pluralistic social existence. It can involve celebrities to deliver such meaningful messages of maintaining communal harmony. Stories of tolerance, trust and understanding between neighbors of different religions abound in different corners of the nation. Tele-series focusing on such human bonding which are more deep and fundamental than the shallow barriers of religion can be played on television and radio to deliver the message of communal harmony.

The power of media, as the voice of a vibrant civil society cannot be snubbed. As the fourth pillar of system, its' constructive role in nation building must be appreciated and utilized in full measure. On one hand it acts as the mirror to the government of the day to rectify the apathy and shortcomings in facilitation, while on other it has the power to influence masses and bring about corrective action. It can be the force multiplier which magnifies goodness and values in the society. Any sort of communal disturbance jolts the society and the nation. As levels of tolerance take a dip in a fast paced society, the role of media in portrayal of events and perception building has a far reaching effect. Any communal disturbance affects the healthy pace of development of the society and the nation. Trade, manufacturing and the economy suffers but worse is the evaporation of trust, affection and understanding between the communities. This vacuum is tough to fill and must be prevented from being created at all. It is here that media must act as a messenger of peace and harmony. It must act as a medium which not only highlights the facts but also rouses the larger question to enable people question the sanctity of such reckless spurts of violence. Media's positive role can be the most significant difference in mitigating damage.

# Part C

# Develop Better Writing Skills

Sharpening the Writing Skills

# Growing *as a* Better Individual

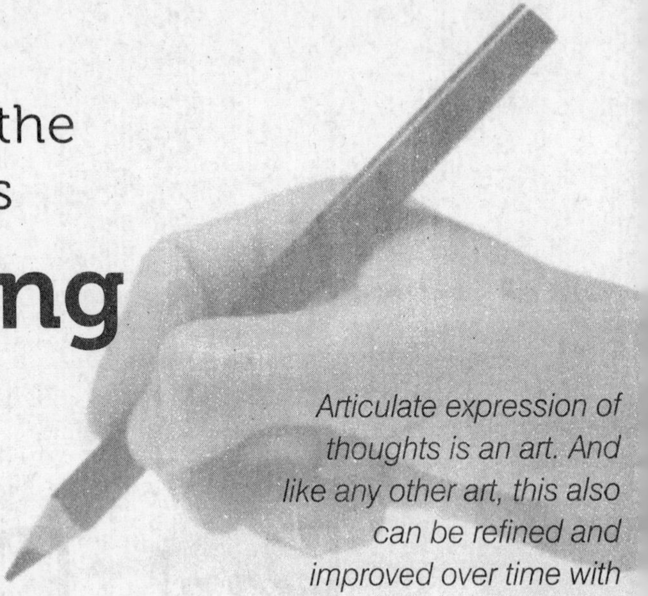

*Articulate expression of thoughts is an art. And like any other art, this also can be refined and improved over time with little sustained effort. The ingredients for such enrichment include*

## Read

A regular reading habit is the most enriching gift one can present oneself. Bring variety to your reading domain. **Start with the newspaper articles and move to essays, stories, novels and books of science, travel, biography, sports, history.** Each gives an insight into the method of organizing and presenting the subject matter. Books fill your mind with fine thoughts, patterns of sentences and methods of articulation. Active reading not only involves the eyes but several regions of the grey matter through the process of continuous imagination. The reader must establish an active connection with the author's world of imagination. As one plays the events on the curtains of mind, he develops faculties untouched by any other activity.

## Observe

Experience is the best teacher. **Look around – see, hear, feel and learn from your own experiences**. These will give depth and dimension, a personal touch to what one thinks and writes. Be alive to life and the experiences of the senses. Try to find expressions that best describe the deepest feelings and emotions. The attempts to read the faces of unknown travelers or demystify the signs of nature give meaningful insights.

To an observant eye, world teems with action and emotion while shades constituting life multiply manifold. And all such nuances generate thoughts, which can be carved through a larger range of words and expressions.

## Think

Better thinking finds immediate reflection in ones writing. Both reading and observing are incomplete without giving them a thought later on. Thinking about the **emotions** and the **feelings** one had experienced brings clarity to the thought process of individual. It helps one see deeper meanings into things. One develops the ability to identify real from fakes - both events and people. Such introspections form the basis of growth of an individual. It helps one to connect with the soul and give deeper meaning to the happenings around him and eventually to his life. I can practice taking out five minutes before bed daily and thinking about the events of the day.

## Write

More one writes, better one writes. **One may write about the people we meet, beautiful scenes, gardens, laughter, tears, joys, journeys, get together or parties.** It may be a taxing experience initially. There will be lot of resistance to even scribble down half a page. However, once this habit of penning down little experiences is ingrained, it becomes the most enjoyable hobby. The person soon develops acumen about selecting experiences worth writing about. One could begin with diary entries or use the widely popular electronic mediums. **Blogging** can also be considered as an option. The appreciation by fellow readers on this platform is encouraging and motivates one to improve further.

> *Reading maketh a full man,*
> *Conference a ready man,*
> *and Writing an exact man.*
>
> —*Bacon*

# Suggested List of **Topics for Practice**

*(A suggested list of relevant topics which can be practiced in the mock sessions before the examination).*

1. Outsourcing : *Trends and Impacts*
2. The Dignity of Labour
3. Third World Industrialization
4. Millennium Development Goals : *The Road ahead*
5. Life of an Illegal Immigrant
6. Corporate Social Responsibility in India : *Evolution and Performance*
7. Streets of My City
8. Habit is Second Nature
9. Reuse Reduce Recycle
10. A Woman in an Indian Metropolitan
11. Growing Intolerance in the Society
12. Wikileaks and the Age of Transparency
13. An Eye for an Eye
14. Tax Avoidance and Tax Havens : *Undermining Democracy*
15. Life of an Anti Corruption Protest
16. The Difficult Indian Neighbourhood
17. The Right to Dissent
18. Unlocking the Potential of Microfinance
19. We live in Deeds, Not in Years
20. Naxal Menace : *The War Within*